Praise for **Unstriving**

"Hustle culture sold us the lie that more effort would lead to more fulfillment. For many, it's led to the exact opposite. *Unstriving* profoundly shifted how I relate to the idea of 'success' and fulfillment, and it helped me find new ways of being in the world. This marvel of a book will impact not just how you work, but how you live, connect, and show up for what matters most. It did for me and I'm endlessly grateful Caleb Campbell was generous enough to share his wisdom and magic with the world. This book will change your life."

—Jennifer Pastiloff, national bestselling author of *On Being Human* and *Proof of Life*

"*Unstriving* is not a book that contains the next big idea that will change your life. It is, rather, a gentle push into the river—where everything that's keeping you from seeing the mystery and marvel of your true self is slowly carried away.

This is cleansing, clarifying, healing, renewing, revelatory, transformative work. Line after line, page after page, these words are heavy with the tender gravity of truth.

While Caleb Campbell writes with remarkable vulnerability about his own healing journey, this book is ultimately less about his story than it is an invitation into your own.

To read *Unstriving* is to experience the fragments of your own story being gently gathered."

—Jonathan Martin, author of *How to Survive a Shipwreck* and *The Road Away from God* and director of the Center for Spiritual Life at DePauw University

"As a recovering overachiever, Caleb Campbell's *Unstriving* is a balm. People often get to the top of the ladder and realize it was perched against the wrong wall. Caleb invites us to do away with the ladder, to pause and get centered within ourselves before we take our next steps. Our souls are shouting, and Caleb is teaching us how to listen."

—Josh Radnor, actor, writer, and musician

"When you're no longer able or willing to live your life as a performance, *Unstriving* is your guide to what comes next. It's a down-to-earth road map to navigate the wilderness of letting go—in a world that only teaches us to hold on—and ultimately, to find the peace and joy that's waiting on the other side of losing everything you thought you wanted."

—Emily McDowell, founder of Em and Friends
and coauthor of *There Is No Good Card for This*

UNSTRIVING

UNSTRIVING

12 Lessons on Authentic Success from a Recovering Overachiever

CALEB CAMPBELL

BENBELLA

BenBella Books, Inc.
Dallas, TX

BENBELLA

BenBella Books, Inc.
8080 N. Central Expressway
Suite 1700
Dallas, TX 75206
benbellabooks.com
Send feedback to feedback@benbellabooks.com

Printed in the United States of America
10 9 8 7 6 5 4 3 2 1

Library of Congress Control Number: 2026014518
ISBN 9781637749487 (hardcover)
ISBN 9781637749494 (electronic)

Editing by Claire Schultz and Sarah Modlin
Copyediting by Shelby Harbour
Proofreading by Karen Wise
Text design and composition by Jordan Koluch
Cover design by Paul McCarthy
Cover image © Adobe Stock / Ubay
Printed by Lake Book Manufacturing

For Kara—Loving you and being loved by you changed my life.
I'm forever grateful the universe brought us together.

Contents

Now that my ladder's gone, I must lie down where all ladders start, in the foul rag-and-bone shop of the heart.

—"The Circus Animals' Desertion,"
William Butler Yeats

INTRODUCTION

"Life is a web of trials and temptations, but only one of them can ever be fatal, and that is the temptation to think it is by further, better and more aggressive living that we can find life."

—Robert Capon

Looking at my bedside table, littered with half-snorted white lines of cocaine and crushed-up sleeping pills, I knew my heart should have stopped the night before. I took a shaky breath, grabbed a glass of water, and began to cry—not soft tears, but body-shaking, can't-catch-your-breath-while-crying tears. This wasn't my first time partying like this, but it was the moment that I realized what was driving my reckless drug use—I was trying to disappear. As I sobbed over the deadly mix of uppers and downers, I knew I truly didn't care if one day I never woke up. And that terrified me.

Of course, my life hadn't always looked like this. Just a few years earlier, I was on national television, in my White over Gray West Point uniform, being selected in the 2008 NFL Draft. I'd followed the plan, stayed disciplined, collected the achievements, and earned the approval of everyone around me. As a young boy growing up in the Texas Panhandle, where they basically hand you a Bible, an American flag, and a football at birth, this moment was the culmination of a lifelong dream. I had made something of myself, and all my hard work should've felt like a reward—but it didn't. My life didn't feel like a gift to enjoy as much as it felt like a burden to carry.

So, how did I get here?

How did I go from achieving my wildest childhood fantasies to this impulsive pattern of self-destruction? From getting everything I thought I wanted to losing myself in the haze of pills and powder, desperately trying to numb myself from a pain I couldn't name, all while brilliantly hiding behind the image of success? Why did each day feel like a battle between the version of me the world expected to see and the emptiness I secretly carried beneath it all?

It didn't happen all at once. Losing yourself is usually a slow drift. It's a slow erosion—a loss of small pieces that make up your sense of self, like your values, your boundaries, and your willingness to tell the truth around what's really going on in your life. You don't always notice each piece slipping away as it happens because it's often small, unassuming experiences. But these instances add up, and they take a toll. You keep showing up and doing what's expected of you, but in the middle of all that effort, you realize that while the scaffolding is still there, the inside feels stripped bare.

And that's what happened to me.

I had spent years collecting all the points I knew how to collect: all-state high school athlete, inducted into the Texas High School Football Hall of Fame, West Point cadet, captain of my college football team, Army officer, NFL draft pick, NFL player. But underneath the accolades and image of success, there remained a feeling of malaise, a nagging dissatisfaction buried deep within my bones. The highs felt muted, and the lows felt endless.

I had mastered the art of performing—of showing up, doing what was expected, meeting the cultural script for success—but I didn't know how to stop striving. A part of me feared that if I stopped, even for a second, it would all fall apart. That fear, and the endless striving, left me with a different type of exhaustion—the type of tired more sleep doesn't solve.

This experience forced me to confront two terrifying possibilities: either I wasn't working hard enough, or there was something intrinsically broken in me. My life felt like quicksand, pulling me deeper into despair. And when I managed to fight my way forward, the goalposts of happiness and fulfillment kept moving farther down the field.

As I sat there crying uncontrollably and staring at the remnants of my shame scattered across my bedside table, I knew my life had hit a breaking point. I could no longer sustain the game I was playing. My endless striving, once the source of my unmatched drive and determination, had become a weight I could no longer carry. It was not only costing me my joy, relationships, and well-being, but it was threatening to cost me my life.

And maybe that's where you are too.

You might not be staring at a nightstand strewn with pills and powder, but you know what it feels like to be maxed out—giving your best every single day and still left feeling unfulfilled. You're burned out from the effort it takes to show up for your life, for your work, and for your people, and yet it doesn't feel as rewarding as you expected. Maybe, like my former self, you still feel as if something is missing—like a hundred-piece puzzle that came with only ninety-nine. While you know how to strive and survive, it's taking a major toll on your life, and something in you can't stop wondering, *Is this really it?*

We're living in a time when more and more people are asking that question. Careers are being reevaluated, priorities are shifting, and even the roles and identities that once felt immutable are being held up to the light. This isn't happening because we've stopped caring, but because we can no longer ignore the cost of the way we've been living. It's leaving us soul tired—the type of tired that isn't solved with a day off, a weekend at the beach, or a new morning routine. No productivity hack or burst of willpower can touch it. The only way forward is getting honest with yourself and asking: *What if the problem isn't me? What if it's the strategy?*

The Unstriving Journey

Deep down, many of us are longing for a new way to live. The old playbook of striving took us this far. It taught us how to push, perform, and stay in constant motion. And in many ways, it worked. It gave us structure, discipline, and even moments of success. But eventually, it stops working—not because we've failed, but because we've outgrown it. What lies ahead isn't another level of achievement. It's a shift in how we move through our lives. A move from proving to trusting. From managing everything to building the capacity to stay present with what is. From building a life that works on the outside to one that also works on the inside.

The restless inner ache so many of us carry isn't a flaw or a lack of gratitude. It's a message from life that something about the way we've been living no longer fits, and that an inner change is asking to take place. This is life's way of nudging us away from an old way of being and toward an inner evolution that reshapes not what we do, but who we are while doing it.

Most of us are stuck living out a version of ourselves that we had to become to survive—each in our own way. Some of us strive by chasing goal after goal, hoping it will finally be enough to achieve *this* one. Some of us strive by suppressing our needs, always staying small, quiet, and out of the way. Some of us strive by holding it all together, being the strong one, the dependable one, the one who never lets anyone down. And others strive by becoming fixers, managing, helping, and making sure everyone else is okay, even when they're not okay themselves.

While these roles may have once given us safety, approval, and belonging, they eventually outlive their usefulness and start to work against us. They were formed around what life required of us at the time—what we needed to do to get by, keep the peace, or earn our place. But as we grow, the roles don't change with us. They keep asking us to respond the same way we always have. That's where the tension comes from. We're no longer the same person, but we're still living from old patterns. The roles once fit because they matched who we were then. Now, they keep pulling us back into habits and behaviors that no longer fit. They're like a Christmas sweater that once fit perfectly but now squeezes in all the wrong places. From the outside, they still look festive, but wearing them feels constricting. In the same way, these familiar roles may still appear authentic on the surface, but they ask us to shrink who we are to stay inside of them.

The unstriving journey begins when we choose to see the

inner version of ourselves clearly, without shame and with compassion, and then find the courage to begin to let it go. That's the turning point where exhaustion gives way to possibility, and life begins to expand in ways we didn't know were available.

Even though it can feel scary to admit the old way isn't working, there is something real waiting on the other side of that honesty—a way of moving through life that doesn't cost you your health, your relationships, or your sense of self. Most of us know how to show up. We're responsible, dependable, and we do what life asks of us. But often, we do it in a way that comes at a cost. We overstep our boundaries, mute what we're feeling, and live in a constant state of tension just to keep going. On the outside, it can look like we've got it all together, while on the inside, things feel fractured. Unstriving makes a different way possible. It allows you to be engaged in your work, your family, and your purpose without having to silence your own needs, override your limits, or betray what you know is true just to keep functioning.

For many people, this shift doesn't begin with a major crisis. It begins with a sense that something isn't lining up. Life looks fine from the outside. They are doing what they set out to do, but the effort it takes to keep everything moving feels heavier than it used to, and the satisfaction they expected never quite arrives. Nothing is obviously wrong, yet something doesn't feel right either.

More and more people are realizing they don't want to keep forcing their lives forward through sheer willpower, urgency, or fear. People are tired of pretending burnout is just part of being ambitious. They want to give their best effort, perform at a high level, do meaningful work, lead teams, raise families, and build beautiful things. But they also want to enjoy the life they're working so hard to build.

I see this all the time in people who look successful on the outside but carry a constant sense of tension and vigilance inside. They are constantly on high alert, bracing for life to fall apart, so they move from meeting to meeting without coming up for air. They push through exhaustion because slowing down feels irresponsible. They tell themselves things will ease up once this season passes, even though every season seems to demand more. They are capable, committed, and doing good work, but carrying it all in a way that leaves them tired and disconnected.

What they want isn't less responsibility or lower standards. They want space to breathe, to feel what's actually happening inside them, to remember who they are beneath the roles and expectations. They want their work to matter, and they want their lives to feel like something they're present for, not just managing their way through.

Unstriving makes this all possible. It moves you off the survival path and onto your soul path—a way of living that feels both successful and deeply satisfying. This book will walk with you in that direction.

It's an invitation for those brave and honest enough to look inward and admit that external success cannot fix internal unrest. It's for those who have learned to measure their worth by what they produce, what they earn, or how well they hold everything together, and who feel the pressure reset the moment the next goal appears. It's for the leader who can't remember the last time work didn't follow them home, the parent juggling roles while running on empty, the creative who keeps pushing for the next level while wondering why it never quite feels like enough.

If you're carrying this ache—a tension in a relationship you don't have the energy to tend to, exhaustion that more sleep doesn't touch, or a fear that slowing down would cause everything to unravel—this book is an invitation to stop managing that ache and begin listening to it, not as a problem to solve, but as the starting point of a different way of living.

This book is not about morning routines or productivity hacks, and it's not for those who want to hide their exhaustion behind a clever framework and call it growth. It's not for those searching for shortcuts. There's no five-step plan, and I'm not promising a sudden breakthrough.

What this book offers is a new guiding principle for your life—one that helps you understand what's happening beneath the surface when old strategies stop working and shows you how to move through the stuck places without forcing change or self-sabotage. *Unstriving* will teach you to listen for what your life is already trying to reveal. You can hear it in the most ordinary things: in the tension that doesn't go away, no matter how hard you push or how much you succeed. In the patterns that keep repeating in your work or relationships. In the exhaustion you carry that no amount of sleep seems to fix. In the thought you keep ignoring that says, "I can't keep doing it this way." *Unstriving* helps you stop overriding those signals and start responding to them with honesty instead of effort.

Over the course of this book, you'll be guided through a process that helps you understand how you got here and what's being asked of you now. You'll see how this pattern first took shape as a survival strategy that shaped your sense of self. You'll name the deeper layers of exhaustion and how they taught you to chase approval, avoid stillness, and measure your worth by what you produce. You'll explore the invitation to cross a threshold, leaving behind what no longer works and stepping into what's not yet clear. You'll meet the emotions you've tried to outrun—grief, fear, shame—and discover that they hold more wisdom than you thought. You'll learn to let go, to trust the disappearance of an old way of being, to stay in the discomfort of uncertainty, and to build an inner steadiness that doesn't depend on circumstances.

As you walk this path, something inside you will begin to shift. You'll no longer see life as a battle to be won. Instead, you'll start to experience a life experience that feels lighter and clearer. The struggle with yourself will ease, and a different kind of movement will begin, allowing you to flow with life rather than fight against it. What once felt like survival will slowly open into the possibility of greater freedom.

That is the promise of the unstriving journey—and it's available to you.

I want you to know that this book didn't come from a single breakthrough experience or some sudden awakening.

It came from years of paying attention, first to my own soul exhaustion, then to what I was seeing in nearly every room I walked into as a keynote speaker. For a long time, I tried to treat that exhaustion as something to manage or push through. But eventually, it became clear that if I kept living the same way, I would keep succeeding at the expense of something I couldn't afford to lose. Over time, I started noticing how many people were carrying the same weight. Some had built lives that looked full and successful but felt empty on the inside. Others were working hard, doing everything they knew to do, and still felt like they were falling short, like no matter how much effort they gave, something just wasn't clicking. They didn't feel lazy or unmotivated; they felt stuck, confused, and tired of wondering if maybe they were the problem.

Welcome to *Unstriving*. I wrote this book to name what I've seen, but also to help you see your life differently.

This book will help you see your life with more honesty and less fear, to recognize exhaustion not as inadequacy but as a signal for transformation, and to trust that feelings of doubt and burnout are not a sign of failure but of a deeper intelligence waking up and pointing you toward a more real way of living. It's not about doing more external work, but about saying yes to deeper internal growth.

If something in you knows that more is possible, but you're tired of trying so hard, this isn't where the story ends. It's where it begins.

This is your journey into a life no longer driven by exhaustion and fear, but fueled by alignment, joy, and a deeper sense of being enough.

Chapter One

STRIVING—A SURVIVAL STRATEGY

You can't initially see what you are looking for because what you are looking for is doing the looking. I am, at least in part, the very thing that I am seeking. That is what makes me seek it.

—The Ancient Perennial Tradition

For children, striving doesn't usually begin as ambition. Ambition implies future goals, identity building, or personal advancement. Most children aren't thinking that way. They're not asking, *How do I become someone?* They're asking, often without words, *What keeps me connected and safe?* For me, this learning experience began on the peewee football field.

I was seven years old, and everything around me felt oversized. The field seemed to stretch forever, the crowd roared louder than I thought possible, and the kids on the other team looked more like giants than second graders. It was the last play of our all-star championship football game, and I knew the ball was coming to me.

I don't remember the name of the play, only the feeling of standing in position, wiping my hands on my jersey, waiting for the snap. When the ball hit my hands, I took off—zigzagging past a few kids, turning toward the sideline, kicking into overdrive, and racing into the end zone for the game-winning touchdown.

Everyone started cheering, but I wasn't paying attention to the noise. I was searching the sidelines for my biggest fan: my mom. When our eyes met, I ran as fast as my tired legs could carry me and launched myself into her arms. I'll never forget the way she smiled at me or the words she spoke—words that would shape how I saw myself and the world around me for decades to come—*"Caleb, I'm so proud of you. You scored the game-winning touchdown. I love you so much."* In that moment, without realizing it, I learned something so simple, yet so profoundly powerful: Effort and performance could earn connection and safety.

Chasing the Glimpse

Since I was young, I've experienced fleeting moments of internal expansion—glimpses of something bigger than myself, more spacious and more alive. They didn't last long, but they always left a mark. In those instances, it was like something inside of me opened up and whispered, "*There's more than this.*" Even though I couldn't name what *this* was, I could feel it in my chest—a deep ache for something greater than the life immediately in front of me, greater than the limits of the small world I knew and the roles already laid out for me.

At that early age, the ache became the fuel for my ambition. I believed I was meant for something bigger than the world I saw around me. But before I could learn how to follow that sense of possibility and deeper longing, I learned how to chase it through performance—leaving me to believe that *more success* was the only way to reach it.

Growing up in the Texas Panhandle, God and football were practically interchangeable. When I scored the game-winning touchdown at the all-star championship game, it wasn't just celebrated; it was treated as *holy*. The only thing that might have topped it was being cast as Jesus in the annual school Christmas play, but I didn't need a stage to feel chosen. Coaches, church leaders, and other well-meaning adults told me God's anointing was evident in my breakaway speed and ability to make big plays on the field. In those periods of performance, my skill at football wasn't only noticed, it was elevated as proof that I was destined for something bigger.

At the time, those words sounded like encouragement. Only later did I realize they had planted a destructive seed—a warped way of seeing myself—that would shape the next twenty-five years of my life. My mother's hug and words of pride were beautiful, an innocent moment between a mother and her son, full of love and celebration. But beneath the joy, something subtle was planted. That was the day I unknowingly began building what I now call my "survival self"—the version of me I believed I had to be to stay safe, accepted, and loved. My achievements weren't just things I had done; they became evidence of who I was and was not.

Over time, I internalized the belief that you're only as good as your last success. And like a river slowly shaping stone, it worked on me. Moment-by-moment, endless water over stone, this personal ideology wore me into who I believed I had to be. I wasn't aware that I was building an identity around success and performance; I just kept trying to earn the safety and validation I got that day. Like most of us, I didn't know I was submitting to a system that would one day wear me away completely.

I just knew it was working right now, when I needed it.

The Survival Strategy

We're all born into the world with our own unique intelligence—an authentic way of moving through life that is open, curious, and alive. At some point, that authenticity gets sidelined in favor of survival. Sometimes it happens all at once, in a sudden moment of loss, rejection, or humiliation. Other times it happens slowly, through small signs that teach us which parts of ourselves are rewarded, and which are ignored, discouraged, or disapproved of. Either way, we learn to sacrifice our most natural selves for the version we believe will keep us safe. That version becomes our survival self—the self we construct to secure what we need most, like acceptance, belonging, and love.

Every survival self carries with it a striving style, or the pattern it relies on to protect the survival self and keep it intact. For some, it shows up as perfectionism—an instinct to make everything flawless so no one can find a crack to criticize. For others, it takes the shape of people-pleasing, avoiding conflict at all costs. Some lean into control, managing every detail so nothing can surprise them.

For me, it was performance. I gathered every accolade, every nod of approval, every record, and every leadership role like pieces of armor. That validation gave me safety, but it also trapped me in a narrative of myself that wasn't the whole story. As encouragement slowly became expectation and ambition evolved into pressure, I wasn't just chasing success anymore—I was outrunning insecurity, self-doubt, and the deep fear of being ordinary. Performance was my way of keeping the survival self alive.

Striving, at its core, is the exhausting and often unconscious attempt to secure our place in the world. It shows up as reaching, managing, fixing, proving, and holding it all together, often becoming the invisible engine behind how we were taught to live. We do it in our jobs to feel valuable, in our marriages to feel close, in our parenting to get it right. We even do it in our bodies, our beliefs, and our prayers, hoping they will finally make us safe, loved, or enough. We were told, directly or indirectly, that if we worked hard enough and held it all together, the life we longed for would be ours.

Like so many others, I wasn't just performing in sports; I was performing everywhere. I chased perfect grades, tried to be the kid who never got in trouble, and worked to be seen as the one with unshakable faith. I wanted teachers, pastors, coaches—anyone whose approval mattered—to see me as enough. And whenever I fell short, I assumed the problem was me.

These strategies don't appear out of nowhere. We don't wake up one day and decide to build them. We absorb them from the worlds we grow up in—parents and siblings, classrooms and locker rooms, pulpits and playgrounds. By the time we're old enough to question them, "Earn your place or risk being left behind" has become the silent mantra of our lives.

We chase grades and approval, promotions and praise, without realizing we're following a script we didn't write. And because the world often pits us against ourselves, defining success through unattainable standards of beauty, hustle, and strength, we live with the fear that we'll never measure up. So, we build a life that strives to close that gap.

This is how striving takes shape as a survival strategy. We don't cling to it out of greediness or insecurity, but out of fear because, in the beginning, it works. It gives us direction, earns us approval, and creates a false sense of moving forward. The trouble is that the same survival self that initially kept us safe eventually becomes the thing keeping us stuck. The striving style that once propelled us, disguised as worthy ambition, begins to define the limits of what we even believe is possible.

Over time, living this way doesn't just shape what you do, but who you think you are. You carry an image of yourself that's been carefully constructed to protect the survival self, an image you may feel you have to maintain at any cost.

The Image Striving Builds

Where I grew up, if you voiced fear or doubt, the answer was often, "Just have more faith." This was a culture where fear and vulnerability weren't met with curiosity or care, but with quick fixes and spiritual platitudes. In response, I did what so many kids do when told their feelings are wrong or unimportant. I buried any fear, any doubt, all the soft and scared parts of me, and learned to look the part. I buried it all and turned to what I knew best—performance.

To an outsider, my football career must have appeared to be a dream come true. From scoring touchdowns in the all-star championship game to earning my place in the Texas Panhandle High School Football Hall of Fame and securing a Division I scholarship at West Point, I consistently stood out as a top performer. As a freshman, I proudly achieved all-conference honors. As a sophomore, I earned national recognition as one of the standout players in my position in college football. After battling a season-ending knee injury in my junior year, I made a powerful comeback, proudly donning the "C" as team captain in my senior season.

It all culminated in a moment that felt like every football player's ultimate dream. I found myself standing under the dazzling lights of Radio City Music Hall in New York City, surrounded by ten thousand screaming fans chanting my name, and "USA, USA, USA," as NFL Commissioner Roger Goodell approached the podium to announce:

"And with the 218th pick of the NFL Draft, the Detroit Lions select Caleb Campbell."

With that, I became the second player ever drafted out of West Point, and the first granted permission to play and serve simultaneously. I had made it to the Promised Land, but what I thought would be overflowing with milk and honey turned out to be something entirely different.

Shortly after the draft, I was interviewed live with at-the-time-ESPN-host Trey Wingo. He looked straight into the camera on national television and said, "Caleb, you're not just another athlete. You're America's athlete. You're about to be a West Point graduate, an Army officer, and now, you're an NFL draft pick." He meant it as a compliment, but what I heard was a warning: Don't screw this up. Don't be weak. Keep it together at all times. So, I smiled for the camera and said all the right things, while inside, something in me froze.

What should have felt like the peak was really just the next level of the same pressure I'd been carrying my whole life—only it had evolved. It was no longer just about pushing myself to become better. Now it was also about protecting the precious image of success I had built. While the sports world was celebrating my story, I was being crushed under the pressure of pretending to be America's athlete. Slowly, my world shrank. I stopped taking risks, avoided anything that might expose me, and prioritized image control over genuine connection with others.

One night during my first training camp with the Detroit Lions, I stepped out of the hotel elevator and ran into Julian Peterson, one of our veteran leaders on the team. It was our first night off, and I was planning to numb the anxiety that had been building over the first couple of weeks of camp. As he passed by, he pulled me aside and said the linebackers, my position group, were headed to a room to watch film and that I should come along. I offered a quick excuse about having plans and meeting someone, but the truth was, I was going to a bar alone.

I wanted to be in that room and be seen as someone who

belonged. But beneath that desire lay a question I didn't know how to confront:

What if I gave everything I had and it still wasn't enough?

I didn't know how to sit with the tension of that unanswered question, so I gave myself an out. I skipped the film session, so if I failed to make the team, I would have something else to blame. I couldn't bear the possibility that my full effort might confirm my deepest insecurity.

This is how image protection functions when it is in control. It encourages us to shrink our world to ensure the image remains unchallenged. We dodge full effort, so there is always an excuse on the table. We maintain close control while keeping connections at arm's length. The relief is genuinely felt in the moment. The cost is a life that only continues to shrink. That night was more than just a missed film session. It was another time I remained small to safeguard the version of myself I believed I needed to survive.

This is what a life of striving eventually becomes. The achievements remain, but the vitality is absent. The true cost isn't just exhaustion; it's the gradual erosion of your identity. You wake up in a life that resembles what you always imagined, yet feels nothing like what you hoped for. That's the burden of the survival self—it guides you along the survival path, ensuring you perform, prove, and protect, but never truly live. Here, questions begin to emerge:

What if the real work isn't about holding it all together? What if the real work is letting go of the version of yourself that was built to survive, so you can finally become the version of yourself that is built to fully live?

The Hunger Beneath the Hustle

When striving finally stopped working, what rose to the surface wasn't laziness or a lack of ambition. It was hunger—deep, insistent, and unignorable. My hunger wasn't a desire for more applause or success, but for something real, something that could actually satisfy. Looking back, I realize that I had been feeding myself with what I now consider surface-level satisfactions.

These are satisfactions that feel good in the moment but disappear when everything becomes still. Titles, recognition, achievements, and the thrill of approval give you a rush, yet they never truly satisfy. They are like sugar—fast, sweet, and ultimately empty. What I was really starving for was something deeper and more substantial. A kind of soul nourishment that doesn't come from what you achieve, but from a deeper connection to yourself and the world around you.

The problem is that when you've spent your whole life chasing what's on the surface, it's hard to believe a deeper satisfaction even exists. All you really know is that you're tired. The goals don't resonate the way they used to, and there's still a subtle ache in the underbelly of your life that success can never touch. That's when I began to realize I was feeding the wrong part of myself.

Psychologists refer to it as the hedonic treadmill. In Buddhism, there is the concept of the hungry ghost—a spirit with a bottomless belly that is always feeding but never full. It's the endless loop of chasing an inner experience through external pursuits. We hit a goal and feel like we've arrived, but soon the thrill fades, and the same restless void reappears.

So many of us live this way, collecting what looks good on the outside in the hope that it will fill the gap we feel on the inside. And some of the time, it seems to work. A new title, a promotion, or a compliment can take the edge off the ache, but the relief never lasts. The hunger always returns, reminding us that the deeper nourishment we crave cannot be found on the surface.

I've seen this pattern show up in leaders who keep saying yes to bigger roles while losing touch with the people they love the most. I've seen it in high performers who reach milestones they once dreamed of, only to feel strangely flat once they arrive. I've seen it in people who are admired, trusted, and successful, yet privately fear that if they slow down, slip up, or stop winning, they'll be exposed and seen as not enough.

In response, we run faster, work harder, and sacrifice more, believing that if we just hold on tighter and give more effort, the experience of the life we long for will finally arrive. But what many of us eventually discover, often through pain, is that no amount of external success can resolve an internal deficit.

When that deficit grows, it is not only our well-being that erodes, but also our capacity to enjoy the very life we have worked so hard to build. The success remains visible to others, but the joy that once fueled us fades. The moments we once longed for finally arrive, but they pass by without touching us. And in some cases, the entire structure collapses.

The hunger I felt, along with the realization that I was nourishing the wrong part of myself, is not unique. As a keynote speaker and coach, I notice it everywhere. People's stories and roles may vary, but the soul exhaustion and persistent inner ache remain constant.

Maybe you've felt it too—the persistent, gnawing sense that something essential is missing, the awareness that beneath the noise, the effort, and the exhaustion, there is a hunger you can't yet name but can no longer ignore. That hunger is the first stirring of a deeper life inside us, a sign that something within is beginning to wake up.

You're Not the Only One

Even in the depths of that soul-sucking cycle, I could still feel something faint but persistent—an inner knowing that life held more. After practice, I would sit alone in my apartment, scroll through my phone, and wonder how I could feel so empty when everything on the outside said I should be fulfilled. But beneath the exhaustion and perfectionism, there was still a flicker. Like a lighthouse cutting through fog, it reminded me that I had not yet arrived at the life I was truly meant for.

That was the most confusing part. I could sense the ache for more, yet I couldn't reach it. The only play I knew to run was to push harder and do more, but it kept failing me.

So, what do we do when we know that there is more to life, more available to us, but we realize that the endless striving for more success won't bring the type of satisfaction that makes our lives truly worth living?

What do we do when we've followed all the rules, played all the games, collected all the points, and still feel like something is missing, but deep down, we know that trying harder is not the answer?

This is my story, as well as the story I've seen in boardrooms, locker rooms, and living rooms. It hides behind professional smiles, impressive résumés, and curated online profiles. We were taught to hustle harder, climb faster, and never stop. Those rules may have helped us succeed on paper, but they also taught us to build lives around an image rather than around what we most deeply need.

It doesn't take long for us to look around at our lives and the world we inhabit to see that something is happening. The world is evolving as outdated systems collapse and collective consciousness shifts. The rules we learned to live by—hustle harder, climb faster, stay strong, and don't stop—aren't holding up as they once did.

You can see it in the executive who finally makes it to the corner office, only to realize that the view isn't what they had hoped it would be. You can see it in the mid-level manager who's been handed yet another resilience training and wonders how much longer they can carry the load without collapsing. You can see it in parents who hold everything together yet feel invisible because no one is holding them. The younger generation no longer chases the dreams their parents sacrificed everything for, having seen where that path leads.

We are waking up to the reality that more achievement will not satisfy the hunger. What we are searching for isn't out there at all. It has been inside us the whole time, waiting beneath the striving and the image we have worked so hard to maintain. The same flicker I once felt is alive in all of us—a refusal to settle.

And this awakening doesn't mean that ambition disappears. Success and achievement still matter, but what matters most is the force that drives them. Is it fear or love? The need to prove our worth, or the certainty of it? Panic or purpose?

The answer shapes everything. Our starting point determines our destination.

A Gentle Invitation

This chapter has outlined a pattern that many of us did not consciously choose but still found ourselves living within. Striving gave us direction, purpose, and drive, but it also left us carrying a life that appeared successful while making us feel like strangers in our own skin. When the cracks began to show, we believed that doubling down and trying harder was the solution.

The unstriving process doesn't begin by getting rid of striving, but by understanding how it shows up in our lives. Each of us developed a particular way of striving that once helped us adapt, succeed, or stay safe. Over time, that same strategy can become outdated, keeping us stuck in patterns that no longer serve us. Bringing awareness to your striving style is the first step toward loosening its grip and doing it differently.

If you'd like a simple way to do that, I've created a short, sixty-second quiz to help you identify your striving style. You can access it at CalebCampbell.me/Unstriving.

Chapter Two

THE INVITATION TO UNSTRIVE

"If you want to become whole, first let yourself become broken. If you want to become straight, first let yourself become twisted. If you want to become full, first let yourself become empty. If you want to become new, first let yourself become old."

—Tao Te Ching

One of the reasons it's so difficult to let go of our survival self is that, for many of us, it's the version that has been celebrated for most of our lives. It's the version that gets affirmed, admired, and welcomed into the room. Over time, we learn which parts of ourselves are most likely to be received, and we lead with those while setting aside the parts that feel messier and more unfinished, even though they are authentically us. Letting go of this way of being isn't just uncomfortable. It can feel like risking the very acceptance we've spent years earning. The approval, the belonging, the sense of being good in the eyes of others all seem tied to staying who we've been. Even when something inside us is asking for change, the cost of listening can feel too high, and that's scary. For me, this came into focus one night at a dinner table with a group of new friends I had just met.

Nights like this have always stirred a strange blend of excitement and unease in me. A part of me always longs to connect and belong, which is exciting. Yet I can't shake the fear that vulnerability could swiftly morph into regret, especially during the drive home as I replay every word I said that night, always questioning if I shared too much.

I was the last to arrive at the restaurant, so I followed the host through a maze of tables until we reached ours—a long, narrow table that could seat eight. I took my seat near the middle, feeling uncomfortable as I scanned the unfamiliar faces and offered a polite smile to break the ice. I hadn't been sitting for longer than ten minutes when, from the far end of the table, a guy raised his voice above the chatter and yelled, "Man, you've got a huge neck!"

The table went still for a split second before the laughter broke out. Soon, everyone turned toward me, waiting for an explanation of why my neck measured close to twenty-one inches. Before I could redirect their attention, someone asked if I played football. That cracked the door, and then all the questions came fast. "What team?" "How long did you play?" "What was it like?" And then came the one question that always eventually comes. "Why aren't you still playing?"

I answered each one as honestly as I could, taking them from the red dirt roads of the Texas Panhandle to West Point, through the NFL draft, into the military, and back again to the NFL. I struggled to keep my voice even and casual as a knot formed in my stomach, growing heavier with each question.

Then, after a pause, one of the guys leaned back in his chair, grinned, and said the words that landed heavier than all the rest: "Man, I want your life."

On the outside, I laughed. On the inside, I sank.

It wasn't the first time I had felt the gap between who people thought I was and who I actually felt myself to be. In that moment, I pulled back into the familiar script I knew would keep me safe. I offered a polished and aspirational version of myself that gave people just enough to be satisfied without risking being fully seen.

The rest of the night, I stayed hidden behind that image. I played the part, smiled when I was supposed to, and answered in ways that left people impressed with my story. I knew how to do it well because I had been doing it for years.

The person they celebrated and the person I was no longer matched. Their applause only made the pain sharper. And somewhere within me, though I couldn't yet name it, I began to sense that I couldn't keep living this way forever.

The False Self We Maintain

Over time, we become skilled at managing the version of ourselves we believe we need to be. At first, it doesn't even feel like a performance. We learn the lines that earn approval and avoid risk, and slowly, without naming it, we begin to live a script instead of a life.

That script works for a while. People admire it, and the world rewards it. But each time we silence the truth rising inside us, something in us shrinks too. We sacrifice pieces of our true selves for acceptance, until the rift between who we are and who we pretend to be becomes impossible to ignore. The longer we deny the truth, the heavier it grows.

And that refusal doesn't just cost us on the inside; it shapes our relationships too.

The false self is often the version that people fall in love with and rely on. Releasing it is, therefore, terrifying. Because if we release it, we risk disappointing the people who count on us to keep playing the part. We risk losing the closeness that was established through performance. We risk being truly seen and not being chosen.

That's why the invitation to let go of striving feels so

daunting. It isn't only about shifting habits. It's about loosening our grip on the very version of ourselves that we, and others, depend on. The survival self that functioned for a time was never designed to endure.

And, when we're not quite ready to let go, life often forces us.

Divine Ambush

There comes a time in every life when something falls apart. A dream dissolves, a perceived certainty vanishes, a relationship ends, or our body betrays us. Maybe it all happens at once, or perhaps it creeps in slowly during a season when the story we've been telling ourselves begins to fall apart.

It's in these moments that the ground beneath us, once so steady and reliable, suddenly gives way. Everything that held us together—our plans, our identity, our belief systems, our willpower, and our sense of control—no longer binds us as it used to.

For some, the break comes through betrayal or heartbreak. For some, it's a diagnosis, a layoff, or the gradual unraveling of meaning until nothing feels alive. Regardless of its form, the common thread is loss. Some losses cradle us softly. Others sweep in like an earthquake, shattering our assumptions of stability.

For me, and many others like me, it was a stark realization

that even after achieving my childhood dream and collecting all the points I was meant to gather, I still felt empty. The intense hunger, along with a profound dissatisfaction, gnawed at me from within. Nothing eased the ache within. That was when I saw past the illusion. I had been taught that success would bring satisfaction, but that was only a half-truth. Regarding the soul, a half-truth is a complete lie.

What I couldn't see then, and have come to understand since, is that collapse is not merely an ending. It is an opening. Collapse shatters the hard veneer of the survival self we worked so hard to maintain. And through those cracks, what we've avoided, ignored, or postponed begins to surface.

It feels cruel, as if the universe is turning against us, yet it is often a sacred disruption. The ground we trusted gives way, and what was once built on survival is shaken loose. In the space that follows, a more honest life has the opportunity to grow.

The challenge is that these invitations rarely arrive looking like beginnings. They come in the form of loss—the story we lived by, a strategy that once worked, or a version of ourselves that once kept us safe. And if we are not careful, we can mistake that loss for failure.

That's what happened to me. Letting go didn't feel like progress. It felt like something within me was dying, with no promise of what would come next. What I couldn't see then was that this experience had a name.

Across various traditions and cultures, it has long been referred to as initiation.

Initiation and the Sibling Generation

The concept of initiation dates back to traditional and Indigenous cultures across the world. Premodern societies organized around elders, ritual, and shared responsibility long before modern society equated maturity with achievement, productivity, and progress. They understood that growth and transformation didn't happen by accident, but with intention. When a young person's adolescent energy began to peak, the elders recognized that it was time for them to leave behind an old identity and step into a new one. Not just for their own good, but for the good of the whole community. These rites of passage were intentionally difficult and uncomfortable. Initiations often involved challenges, rituals, and periods of isolation, all symbolizing the death of the old self and the emergence of something new.

As a result, it wasn't uncommon for those being initiated to return to their communities with a new name to honor the fact that they had outgrown their former identity. As they no longer identified with who they once were, their new name now represented the calling in their lives and their role within the larger community of their tribe, as well as in the more-than-human world.

Today, most of us never receive that kind of guidance. We don't have elders walking us through sacred thresholds. There are no intentional initiations to help us leave behind our adolescent ways of being. So we grow older, but we don't necessarily grow up. We collect milestones like degrees, jobs, houses, and families, but we never confront the parts of ourselves that are still grasping for validation, pretending or afraid to be fully seen.

As a result, we have grown adults who are trapped in what Robert Bly, the American poet and author of *The New York Times* bestseller *Iron John*, calls a sibling generation. It's a term that describes a culture where adults may appear grown on the outside but remain tethered to adolescent ways of thinking and being. In a culture where we have bypassed true initiation into adulthood, we remain stuck in a perpetual state of striving and self-interest. Instead of stepping into a more grounded and expansive way of being, we're stuck playing a child's game, consumed by comparison, competition, and the endless chase for more to fill the void inside. We believe it will somehow make us whole, but it doesn't. This isn't growth. It's stagnation dressed as success. And as long as we remain tethered to these adolescent ways of being, we deny ourselves the wisdom, depth, and freedom that come from stepping into a fuller, more authentic version of adulthood.

You can see the effects of this pattern almost anywhere—at work and at home. We cling to the same tired games of posturing and proving while avoiding the messier work of becoming whole. I know because I spent years measuring my worth by what I achieved. Not because it fulfilled me, but because I was terrified of falling behind. I needed to be someone special so that other people would approve. This is the hallmark of a sibling generation—individuals who, lacking initiation, have yet to navigate beyond the shores of life into the deeper waters of wisdom, soul purpose, and fulfillment.

And here's the thing: Adolescence isn't bad. It's a natural and necessary stage of life. As I'm writing this, my three-year-old daughter is full of adolescent energy, as she should be. She's constantly vying for her mom's attention by trying to outshine her little brother, all the while incessantly looking for my validation. This is a normal part of the adolescent cycle. How many of us, though, as fully grown adults, are still vying for attention, trying to outshine others, and endlessly seeking validation? How many of us are still trying to prove our worth to bosses, partners, peers, and even strangers online? We've learned how to mask it well, calling it ambition, hustle, or "having a brand." But beneath it all is the same adolescent energy, craving to be seen, loved, and hopefully, one day, enough.

Here's the deeper cut. This endless adolescent behavior isn't just exhausting us; it's also robbing us of the very life we're working so hard to attain. No amount of external success will ever help us see what's already within us. No promotion, no applause, and no amount of approval will ever help us see that our treasure—our inherent worth, our wholeness, our enoughness—has been there all along, waiting for us to stop striving long enough to remember.

As a result, we ultimately find ourselves at war with our lives, constantly seeking something outside ourselves to fulfill a role it was never meant to play. When you struggle against your life for long enough, you eventually become your own worst enemy.

Even in the absence of formal rites of passage, life still manages to tap us on the shoulder. It sends moments that begin to strain the life we've built, making the old way feel increasingly uncertain and less sustainable. These moments arrive in all shapes and sizes, like a growing heaviness in the work you used to love, a subtle distance between you and the people closest to you, or a gnawing discontent with life even though you have every reason to be grateful.

You may not initially see them as initiations. However, if you pay attention, you'll notice a pattern. They start small, build gradually, and eventually you can't avoid what your life is asking of you.

The Little Boy at the Concert

Shortly after I met my wife, Kara, she invited me to a friend's concert. This night was significant not only because her friend was showcasing her talent, but also because I would be demonstrating my potential as "a keeper" to all her friends. I felt vulnerable. At that time, the opinions of others weighed heavily on me, and to make the stakes higher, I already knew that I was in love with Kara. I felt a spark between us that I had never experienced before, but there was a part of me that was afraid that if her friends didn't approve, it would jeopardize what we had.

Despite my inner work, I still struggled to offer safety to the scared little boy within me—the one who felt vulnerable and couldn't ask for reassurance without somehow pretending he didn't need it. So, I turned to familiar adolescent patterns and behaviors when I felt vulnerable. I drank—too much, too fast.

If you have the privilege of knowing my wife, you know she has an electrifying energy about her. It was the first thing I noticed about her when I saw her from across the room the night we met at a writers' retreat in Kentucky. She effortlessly glided from person to person, engaging in conversations and radiating a type of joy that makes your heart smile. That night at the concert, she was in her element, and it drew people in just as it had first drawn me in. She wasn't doing anything wrong; she was just being herself. But as the night went on, my drinking wasn't just dulling the vulnerability I felt while being surrounded by new people; it was fueling a deep jealousy and growing insecurity in relation to her.

At that time, I lacked the awareness to understand what was happening within me, much less the tools to communicate it. I couldn't articulate my needs, and I lacked the language to express the fears of the little boy that influenced much of my behavior. I grew up in a home where emotions weren't expressed, and intimacy wasn't demonstrated. My parents did their best with what they had, but we struggled to be emotionally close. When it came to emotions, we only knew how to control or suppress. So, I learned to seek connection in the only way I knew—by creating chaos.

Throughout my early adult relationships, I would pick fights or stir up conflict anytime I needed connection, not because I wanted to hurt anyone, but because I was desperate to feel a sense of closeness with the person I was dating. So, if I could provoke a reaction, maybe we would move toward a repair. And for a moment, in the tension and release, I felt something that resembled intimacy and connection. It wasn't genuine intimacy, but it was the closest I knew how to achieve. This was a familiar cycle that I had experienced in every relationship I had ever had. And here it was again, on full display. It would take me some time beyond that night to realize that what I had once thought of as love was actually just a survival strategy disguised as love.

As the night progressed, I began to pull back. My answers to Kara's questions became harsh and brief. When she wanted me to meet someone, I told her to go ahead without me. "I'll be fine," I said, even though I wasn't. The booze was a hidden store of gasoline in my body, and the jealousy and insecurity building throughout the night became the spark that set me on fire and almost burned this newfound love down to the ground. The whole drive home consisted of me bombarding Kara with endless questions about this guy or that guy. I wanted to know every little detail about the history of their friendship and, luckily, I somehow managed to convey it in a way that made me sound logical. Over the years, I had learned how to position my insecure questions in a way that emotionally manipulated the situation, so I wasn't seen as the bad guy.

The intensity of my questions was evidence of my love, and my incessant need to know reflected my burning desire to be able to love better. But it was all little boy energy.

And, thankfully, Kara saw right past all of it.

Somewhere around 3 AM, Kara let me know in no uncertain terms that if I didn't grow up and learn how to meet the needs of the little boy inside me, what we had was over. She refused to be in another relationship with a man who was still trapped in his own adolescence. And for the first time, I truly heard this message. Her boundary was clear, and it forced me to see that the very patterns that once kept me safe were now destroying my chances of getting what I most wanted. That night wasn't just a relational wake-up call, but a divine ambush—the collapse of a self I could no longer drag into my future.

Sometimes, this is what initiation looks like. It meets us in the mess, in the collapse of the strategies we've relied on, and forces a choice: Cling to the false self or begin to become someone new.

Choosing What Dies

Recently, I rewatched a show on HBO Max called *Industry*. It follows a group of ambitious young graduates hustling to break into the high-stakes world of investment banking in London. Later in the series, one of the lead characters, Yasmin, decides to walk away from it all—her status, her role, and her place at the table. Everyone around her is confused. Why leave behind what others are still fighting so hard to keep? And then she says something unforgettable: "I knew that if I left, a part of me would stay forever. But I knew that if I stayed, a part of me would leave forever."

When I first heard those words, it felt as though someone had taken the feeling I'd carried for years and put it into a sentence. They weren't just about a character in a show; they were about all of us. Because there comes a point when staying costs more than leaving. It's the moment you can no longer pretend, when keeping things as they are feels heavier than risking change. You may not know what's next, but you can feel what cannot continue.

That recognition is the beginning. The shape of your life might still look intact, but inside, you sense the foundation shifting. Something will have to give. If we stay tethered to an outdated way of being, what slowly dies is our authenticity, our aliveness, and our capacity to become who we were meant to be. This is the sacred tension unstriving leads us into—a choice.

Will you stay, allowing a deeper part of you to slip away quietly over time? Or will you walk toward what's real, even if it means letting go of everything that once made you feel safe? The point is, death is inevitable. If we remain the same, something will die. If we choose to let go, something will die. The courageous choice is to choose the death that empowers you, not the one that holds you back.

What will you let die? This is the choice we're invited to make. Our work is learning how to embrace this choice.

A Gentle Invitation

If this chapter brings up memories of times when you've held back, I invite you to gently test those edges—not by forcing change, but by noticing where you're still protecting an image of yourself that once kept you safe.

This week, choose one area of your life where you regularly feel the gap between who you present yourself to be and what's actually true. To bridge that gap, experiment with letting a little more of the truth *out*. This could be as simple as answering a "How are you?" with something real or sharing an honest detail you'd usually keep tucked away, instead of sticking to the same safe script.

As you make this simple change, pay attention to what happens inside you. Do you feel relief, fear, or the urge to retreat? These reactions aren't signs you're doing it wrong—they're signs you're becoming someone new.

To be clear, this isn't about fixing yourself or oversharing. It's about practicing the kind of honesty and authenticity that allows an outdated way of being to fall away. Because every small act of truth prepares you for the bigger changes that transformation will eventually require—a rehearsal for the larger letting go.

Chapter Three

CROSSING THE THRESHOLD

Before you start the journey, you own the journey.
Once you step into the journey, the journey owns you.
– Old Proverb

When I had just signed with the Kansas City Chiefs, it felt as if the stars had aligned for the first time in my NFL career. The general manager of the team believed in me, I felt connected to the players, and the city felt alive. This was the moment I had been chasing since I was just a young boy, and now it was finally here. The football gods were finally smiling down on me.

One afternoon, after one of my first practices with the team—and a practice where I played *well*—I was struck by something I couldn't ignore. Even here, even now, after finding myself in the middle of the success I had chased my entire life, I didn't feel the way I thought I would.

The entire team had gathered in the film room so we could watch the practice session together. These sessions were always vulnerable because the practice tape doesn't lie. Every move, on and off the field, gets analyzed. This time, however, I wasn't worried—I had played well. This should've been a moment of pride and joy.

But when the meeting ended, and the team began to clear out, I remained seated. I told myself I just wanted a moment to take it all in, but really, I was trying to understand why I still felt so uneasy.

All my efforts had led me here. The dream I had pursued since boyhood was finally mine, yet the relentless tension in my body hadn't eased. The fear, the pressure, and the silent panic I had carried from city to city, team to team—they were all still with me. I had always believed that if I landed on the right team, with the right people, and played good football, all my inner turmoil would finally settle. But here I was, in that right place with those right people, and nothing felt settled.

I discovered that the goal posts of satisfaction had only moved farther away. The exhale I longed for never came. And the way I was living—perfecting the facade and chasing the edge of bigger, faster, stronger at all costs—was taking its toll.

I could no longer reconcile my success with the inner deficit I felt. And while it would take time to summon the courage to walk away from my childhood dream, I could feel that something essential had shifted. The illusion I'd been living under had lost its authority. The life I was living no longer fit the person I was becoming, yet I had no sense of what came next.

Threshold Moments

Although I didn't have the language for it then, I was standing in the middle of a threshold moment—a pivotal realization that came later.

A threshold moment is that turning point when the story we're living stops serving us. When our strategies, our professional and domestic roles, everything we've built to hold our lives together and move forward, can no longer carry the weight of who we're becoming. And in that moment, even if nothing breaks on the outside, something shifts on the inside.

While some threshold moments come from a complete collapse, others arrive in our lives through more subtle shifts. You might not be able to name *it*, but you can feel *it*. There's a frustration that gnaws at you—a frustration that, when you stop trying to outrun it or outperform it, has the power to transform how you relate to your life entirely. Your body brims with discontent because things should feel better than they do. A voice inside you begins to stir, and you can't ignore it any longer. You find yourself going through the motions of a life that looks fine on the outside but no longer feeds you on the inside. When you reach a moment like that—whether in your work, your relationships, or your sense of self—you've arrived at a threshold.

The thing about thresholds is that they don't come with a plan or an indication of what comes next on the other side. What they do is make it impossible to keep pretending on this side, nudging you to move forward. They slow you down and quiet the distracting noise of striving. They hold you in that in-between place—no longer who you were, not yet who you're becoming.

These moments are not solely personal either. They appear in narratives that cultures have shared for centuries to describe moments when life no longer functions as it once did.

For example, Arthurian legends tell the tale of a once-prosperous kingdom that has fallen into ruin. The rivers have dried up, the trees no longer bear fruit, and the land has become barren. Everything is suffering, not because of war or famine, but because the king has been wounded.

The deeper truth of the story is that the kingdom is only as healthy as the king. The land reflects the condition of his soul. But no matter how much wealth, medicine, or praise he receives, nothing heals him—nothing external can touch the internal wound. So, the land remains dry, and the people remain lost. Until, one day, a traveler comes along and, instead of offering a gift, simply asks the question that no one else has asked:

What ails thee, my king?

That question changes everything. Not because it fixes the wound, but because it allows the wound to be seen. And seeing, in moments like these, is the first step across the threshold.

I think about that story often because I've lived it. And so have most people I've worked with. We high achievers tend to build lives that work, if only for a short time. Some of us even build lives that look like they are thriving. But underneath, something feels dull. Joy dries up, and our energy becomes brittle. We find ourselves enduring our lives by going through the motions. Outwardly, it may still look impressive, but inwardly, something is no longer connecting. The old strategy that worked for so long starts to fall apart.

That moment, when life starts to feel strangely empty or uninhabited, is its own threshold. And like the king, the question that opens the door is not, "How do I fix this?" but rather, "What is really happening inside me?"

Crossing the threshold into a new way of being doesn't begin when you have all the answers figured out; it begins the moment you're honest about what's no longer working, even if you don't fully understand it yet.

Folktales and legends show that thresholds involve more than just solving problems or reaching greater goals. They are opportunities in our lives to confront our inner reality and allow ourselves to change.

This is the essence of initiation. Initiation, whether it's brought on by an intentional ritual like a rite of passage or the chaos of life, requires us to let go of our old selves and allow someone new to emerge.

Life's Initiations

Life initiates us more often than we realize. And even when we choose them, moments of initiation are always disruptive. In some way, small or large, they interrupt the life we knew and strip away familiar rhythms and identities. You're being asked to release who you've been so that someone new can emerge.

In the past, elders and rituals helped people recognize and move through these turning points. Most of us didn't grow up with that kind of guidance, but the need for transformation didn't disappear. So, initiation still comes, often without warning or context. Sometimes it comes through loss—a diagnosis, betrayal, breakdown, or an inner discontent we can no longer ignore. Sometimes it comes through expansion—receiving a promotion that carries greater responsibility or stepping into a relationship that asks us to be seen in deeper ways. In both cases, the effect is the same. The life we were living can no longer continue as it was because we are no longer the same. This is what makes these moments different from ordinary hardship. Hardship strains the life you're living. Initiation dismantles the self you've been living from.

Saying yes to this work isn't easy. It often feels like a kind of death, because it is. There is often the loss of identity, of control, of everything that once gave us meaning. But beneath that death is a strange form of liberation. Because when the life you've built stops being sustainable, it's freeing to let it go.

Psychotherapist, writer, and soul activist Francis Weller calls these unavoidable moments soul initiations. They are the moments when life breaks the structure you've been living in and asks you to reorganize from the inside out. The inner compass you've been using loses its accuracy, forcing a new way of orienting your life. This doesn't come as a punishment for some kind of wrongdoing. Rather, it's a preparation for what will be.

The ancient alchemists carried a similar belief. While known for turning base metals into gold, alchemy was also seen as a mirror for the refinement of the soul. At its heart was the belief that inside every living thing is an indestructible essence that survives fire, loss, and collapse.

They called it the scintilla—the spark. In alchemy, this is the hidden seed that endures no matter how much the exterior shell is burned away. In the human soul, it shows up as an ember that cannot be extinguished. You can lose the job, the health, the marriage, even the self you've spent years perfecting, and still the spark will remain. When everything else has fallen away, it is often the first warmth you feel in the dark. It does not give you a map forward, but it does remind you that life itself has not abandoned you.

That's what initiations do. They strip away the borrowed identities and survival strategies until only the ember remains—the part of you that cannot be destroyed, even when the life you knew no longer exists.

I used to think initiation had to be dramatic or overtly spiritual, but now I have come to see it woven into the fabric of life. I saw it when my wife labored for sixty-three hours before becoming a mother. I recognized it in the silence that followed a client's career ending before they were ready, and the slow grief of a relationship coming to an end. I've felt it in the deep sadness of losing a job I had poured myself into. Initiation is present in every moment that remakes us at the identity level—when the version of you that got you here can no longer support the life that's now unfolding.

These moments, though they look different on the surface, move us through the same inner terrain and follow a similar pattern with three consistent traits.

First, there's a severance from the world you once knew. What was once familiar no longer fits, and the door behind you is closed. Then, there's a shift in identity. You are no longer who you were, and it's not just your roles that are changing. It's your sense of self. Finally, there's a realization that you can't go back. The old way isn't just gone; it's over. If you want to keep going, you have to become someone new.

Parenthood is one of the clearest examples of this. In an instant—or after sixty-three hours of labor, as in my wife's case—your identity shifts. You are no longer only yourself but also a caretaker, protector, and nurturer. Familiar routines are replaced by new responsibilities that stretch you in ways you never imagined. It is a severance from one world, a radical alteration of identity, and a realization that there is no return. If you allow it, parenthood initiates you into a deeper, more expansive life.

But initiation is not limited to parenthood. It is universal.

You can see it in the service member who hangs up the uniform and suddenly must navigate a world that no longer reflects the purpose and identity they once carried. You can see it in the mid-level manager laid off after decades in the same role, untethered from the stability they once trusted. You can see it in the athlete who wakes up to silence—no locker room, no game-day rituals, no crowd—and is left to wonder who they are without the performance.

Anyone who has faced a major transition, loss, or unexpected change knows this terrain of initiation. And because formal rites of passage are absent in modern life, we lack the framework to understand them. So, we cling to the old scripts—be bigger, faster, stronger, more successful—because they feel safe, even when they no longer serve us. Our instinct is to power through, fix, and move on. But initiation asks the opposite. This is not a place to push harder. It is a place to soften, to build inner strength by learning to sit in the discomfort long enough for something new to emerge.

In this space, answers can't be forced through control. They come slowly, not through force, but through allowing. And as we wait in the threshold space, we are changed, not in spite of the unknown, but because of it.

While the invitation to initiation is always present, it is up to us to find the courage to accept it. And that "Yes" rarely comes easily. Staying in the discomfort of the in between, without rushing for a resolution, demands more of us than we might expect. It confronts the very strategies we've relied on for survival.

And even when we sense that something new is possible, the pull of the old story can be strong. Psychologists call this loss aversion—our tendency to fear what we might lose more than we trust what we might gain. When identity is on the line, that fear can keep us tethered to lives we've already outgrown. So, we hesitate, delay, and resist the very change we know we need—until life intervenes.

Resisting the Initiation

I knew I should have walked away from the NFL long before I did, but I was too afraid. Not afraid of starting over, but of letting go. Letting go of the identity I had constructed my entire life around—the status, the structure, the narrative that being a football player defined for me.

So, I stayed.

I stayed in a game that was no longer mine to play. I kept showing up, performing, pushing, trying to keep a version of my life intact that was no longer meant for me. That's the thing about initiations. You can resist them, but that doesn't make them go away. If anything, it just makes the experience more painful. I learned this the hard way.

One day, long after I knew it was time to leave the NFL, I was driving on a busy road with the sun in my eyes. I misjudged a turn and was T-boned at an intersection. My car spun around twice before wrapping around a telephone pole. Thankfully, the impact hit the rear passenger side, just far enough from where I was sitting to avoid serious injury. I was able to get away with only a few cracked ribs and cuts, but the wreck shook me in a way nothing else had.

I had been living in the low hum of denial, staying busy enough to not look too closely, ignoring the invitation to begin again. But now, there was no more hiding. With my ribs cracked and my body forced into rest and stillness, I could no longer distract myself from the truth I had been avoiding.

My heart had already left the field, but I hadn't yet said yes to what was next. I was still clinging to the version of myself I wanted to be, hoping I could bypass the uncertainty and land somewhere solid. But that's not how it works. Thresholds don't offer shortcuts—they demand surrender.

Inner Spaciousness

When I finally began to let go, something unexpected happened. Beneath the grief, fear, and uncertainty, a spaciousness began to open up in my life. It reminded me of walking into my grandmother's house a few days after Christmas. During the holidays, every inch of her house was covered with tiny ornaments on the shelves, decorations hanging from the doorways, snowmen on the end tables, and bowls of candy on the counter. And the Christmas tree? It could rival the one from Chevy Chase's *Christmas Vacation*: big, bright, and taking up half the living room. The house felt packed. Warm, but so full you almost had to turn sideways to get through the clutter. But walking into my grandmother's house a few days after Christmas was a different experience. The tree was gone, and the garland was packed away. At first, the room felt bare. But then, I noticed it also felt bigger. There was more air, more light, and more room to breathe.

That is the gift of initiation. Not an immediate sense of clarity, but space. It clears out the clutter of who we were so that there is space for who we are becoming. Without that space, growth has nowhere to land. When we cling to what no longer fits, we block the very room we need. We stay crowded by what was meant to be released.

What often follows is an unfinished crossing. We reach a threshold but refuse to step through, or we step into change but refuse to be changed by it. Life still looks intact on the outside but feels restless and brittle to those within it. Burnout, despair, and aimlessness often signal a threshold we've reached but failed to cross. We paused, postponed, or plowed ahead, preventing the inner shift and halting the transformation.

The hard truth is that you can't resolve an unfinished crossing by starting a better morning routine, escaping to the beach for a weekend, or leaning on a new productivity hack. This isn't an optimization problem. It's a surrender problem.

The only way through is to cross over the threshold. You have to stop trying to hold everything together. You must release the version of life that no longer fits. And you must say yes to where you are, even without knowing where it leads.

As the resistance softens, spaciousness will return. A spaciousness that becomes the fertile soil needed for new life to grow.

Emily's Threshold

I met Emily when I first moved to LA. At the time, she was the founder of a fast-growing stationery brand with thousands of devoted fans. "There was an inordinate amount of press attention," she told me once.

From the outside, she was living the dream that many entrepreneurs aspire to. But as our friendship grew, I began to see the deeper story beneath the polished surface. The story no one else could see: Emily was drowning under the crushing weight of success.

In her own words, she revealed the pressure she was living under. The success she worked so hard to build became the weight that began to fracture her life.

> *"I felt crushed under the weight of expectations: our customers', the team's, my own. The biggest, by far, being my own. I believed that I should be able to rise to the occasion and live this life that everyone told me was a dream, and that if I couldn't make it work, something was wrong with me."*

Emily had reached the pinnacle of success, but it exacted a price. Her old life and identity couldn't propel her into the future she desired.

Like so many of us, she didn't yet have a name for what was happening. Because when success begins to hollow out your life, and your dream starts feeling less like something to enjoy and more like something you have to endure, it's hard to tell the difference between failure and opportunity.

Emily didn't realize it at the time, but she had reached a threshold moment. The life she had built could no longer be held by her current way of being. The strategies that once worked were no longer working. Though the exterior appeared intact, the interior told a different story. Not due to any inadequacy as a leader or person, but because something deeper within her was asking to come alive.

Not long after this conversation, when I heard that she had sold the company and stepped away from the role she had spent years building, it clicked. Sustaining her life on willpower alone ended up costing her too dearly. Like Yasmin in the show Industry, she had reached the moment where holding on was costing her more than letting go—what she had to release wasn't just the company itself, but her grip on what success was supposed to mean. The version of winning she had been conditioned to chase had to go so that her own definition could finally take its place. Crossing a threshold often requires this.

She severed ties with her old world, experienced a profound shift in identity, and realized she could never return to the way things were. Despite not knowing what lay ahead, she embraced the leap, leaving behind a life that no longer served her and made room for the tension of unanswered questions.

What shifted wasn't just her role or her address. It was who she thought she had to be. The relentless pressure to uphold an image and justify a life that no longer fit fell away. She no longer needed success to validate her worth or prove she was strong by staying. The center she had been living from gave way to something truer, even as the future remained unclear.

Emily didn't just change her circumstances. She let herself be transformed.

And to be clear, saying yes to your threshold moment doesn't always mean quitting your job, leaving your marriage, or relocating to the other side of the world. Sometimes it means staying exactly where you are and doing the harder thing: Living more honestly, shedding old roles, and patiently listening for what comes next.

That's what Emily's story really reflects. Not a change in scenery, but a change within.

A Gentle Invitation

If you've been feeling disconnected from your own life—going through the motions, sensing something in you is fading—you may be standing at a threshold. It might show up as a shift in your role, a change in your energy, or the sense that what once worked no longer does.

Thresholds rarely respond to more effort or willpower. They are not puzzles to be solved, but open doorways to be entered. Sometimes the most courageous thing we can do is pause long enough to notice the invitation they hold.

So, take a breath. Let the questions rise gently: *What threshold might I be standing at? What is life asking me to release? What am I still holding that I know is ready to be set down?*

This is how we begin to create the much-needed inner spaciousness within our lives to continue the unstriving journey.

Chapter Four

HIDING IN THE HUSTLE

"It's not the sadness that sinks a person's life. It's the energy a person spends avoiding sadness that sinks a person's life."

—*Barbara Brown Taylor*

We all have our hiding places. For some, it's at the bottom of a bottle. For others, it's found in the refuge of a relationship. For me, it was in the endless hustle, always striving for something more. When I say "hustle," I don't just mean working hard. I mean the constant need to prove, to perform, to keep moving so fast no one notices the parts of you that you'd rather not face. The parts that feel small, broken, or not enough.

I started hiding long before I ever put on an NFL jersey.

I don't remember exactly how old I was, only that I was still young enough to believe adults would always protect me. It was a crowded day at my grandma's house. The living room overflowed with relatives, laughter spilling from room to room. I remember weaving between people, sidestepping knees and trays of food, when a relative pulled me aside to ask a question. What I didn't realize was that I had also stopped right in front of my uncle, who had been drinking Coors Original since that morning.

Without warning, he reached out and yanked my pants down in front of everyone. There I stood—fully exposed—while he erupted in laughter loud enough to capture the room. I don't remember what I was wearing or how people looked at me. But I do remember the sound, the roar of laughter swallowing me whole.

Before my mind fully recognized what was happening, my body knew what to do. I frantically pulled up my pants, turned and ran as fast as I could, out the door, across the yard, and into the barn where I buried myself behind a pile of hay bales. Hours passed before anyone came looking for me, but by then, the damage had already been done.

It wasn't just embarrassment I carried away from that day—it was a toxic belief that whispered, "If you see the real me, all of me, you'll see I'm not enough." From then on, I learned to protect myself the only way I knew how—by hiding. Not behind hay bales this time, but behind performance, productivity, hard work, long hours, and being the first in the gym and the last to leave.

On the outside, it looked like drive, ambition, even inspiration. On the inside, I was still that terrified boy sprinting out of the room, fully convinced that if anyone ever saw the real me, they would also see the full extent of my inadequacy.

For me, being fully seen meant being exposed. That belief became my fuel. It meant I pushed harder than anyone else because achievement felt safer than intimacy, and proving myself felt less risky than being myself.

And for a time, that fuel sustained me. That's the thing about shame, fear, self-doubt, insecurity, and any other uncomfortable inner experience—they're incredible motivators. They'll convince you that if you can just do enough, be enough, achieve enough, you'll stay protected.

Unfortunately, no matter how fast or how far you run, they'll run with you. And over time, the hustle that once felt like a tool for building your life will turn into a shield—keeping you safe from exposure but also keeping the goodness of life at arm's length. On the outside, your drive still looks like ambition. On the inside, it's a full-time effort to outrun the very parts of yourself and your story that most need to be seen, heard, and healed.

America's Fixation on the Hustle

America's fixation on relentless work and productivity is nothing new. It's woven into the fabric of our national identity and stitched into the very seams of that hopeful thing we call the American Dream. From the beginning, we were told that with enough hard work, enough sacrifice, and enough hustle, anything was possible.

A 1914 job ad from *The Chicago Defender* described delivering newspapers as an "easy task" for "any wide-awake boy with a little hustle in him." Hustle was framed as not just admirable, but essential. It was the mark of a good citizen, a worthy man, a person destined for greatness.

By the 1980s and beyond, technological advancements promised boundless opportunities, and entrepreneurial success stories became the new American gospel. The hustle mentality wasn't just celebrated; it was glorified. Figures who rose from garages and dorm rooms to billion-dollar empires have become modern-day saints. Productivity was no longer about survival; it had become a badge of honor. To be busy was to be important, and to be exhausted was to be doing something right.

In more recent years, entrepreneurs like Gary Vaynerchuk have helped usher in a new era, where the daily grind isn't just something you endure as much as it is something you broadcast. The rise of vlogging culture magnified the hustle culture even further. Suddenly, it wasn't enough to be grinding behind the scenes. Now, you had to show it. You had to prove it.

Your effort had to be witnessed to be validated. With a camera following him nearly 24/7, Gary documented early-morning flights, back-to-back meetings, late-night brainstorms, and the thin sliver of sleep in between. He didn't just talk about the hustle. He made it visible, tangible, and most importantly, aspirational.

For some of us, hustle isn't just fuel. It's oxygen. In a culture where worth is earned and belonging is conditional, the pursuit of more feels like the only way to stay ahead of the ache of not being enough. The scarcity inside us has turned pain into productivity, and for a time, that productivity can be life-giving. It can even feel like purpose.

There's an older meaning tucked inside the word *hustle* that's largely been lost in today's culture. Its original meaning didn't point first to urgency or effort, but to a posture of obtaining by begging. Hustle trains us into that posture. We move through life as if what we're searching for—safety, belonging, worth—exists somewhere outside of us, just out of reach. So, we strive, we prove, and we perform. The hustle convinces us we're beggars asking for scraps when, all along, we're standing on a treasure we don't recognize as our own. We keep appealing outward for what was never missing in the first place.

The danger comes when the hustle becomes your lifeline. When your sense of self and worth is so entangled in your productivity that you can't afford to stop, because stopping might mean confronting the very thing that you've been running from—yourself.

The Letter That Changed Everything

Shortly after the NFL draft, I went through a season where I received a flood of fan mail. Letters came in from all over the country. People would congratulate me, tell me how much they were rooting for me, or share how meaningful it was that a West Point cadet would now be representing their family in the NFL. Some were veterans. Others were proud sons and daughters of veterans.

Several of the letters included my rookie card and asked for a signature—sometimes for themselves, sometimes for their kids, sometimes for friends or family members battling cancer in the hospital. I tried to read every letter I could. Most of them made me feel supported, and for a while, they made me feel special.

But there was one letter I'll never forget.

It arrived in a plain 8x11 envelope. Inside was a photo of Pat Tillman—former NFL player turned Army Ranger who had left football to serve after 9/11 and was later killed in Afghanistan. At first, I felt pride that my name, in some small way, might be mentioned near his. But when I unfolded the letter, the pride vanished. A pit formed in my stomach as I realized almost instantly that this wasn't fan mail but hate mail.

The letter was long and scathing. The man accused me of disrespecting the military, called me a fraud and a coward for choosing to pursue the NFL after graduation. He shared, in graphic detail, how his son's best friend had been burned alive in a Humvee explosion and how his son had to scrape his friend's remains into a body bag. He said I didn't deserve to wear the same uniform patch as the men who had given their lives. That I wasn't a real soldier, just a protected and coddled athlete.

He ended the letter by telling me to walk to the West Point cemetery, stand in front of every headstone, and explain how I intended to carry the same weight they once did. "You had a C on your uniform," he wrote. "I always thought that stood for captain, but in your case, it's appropriate—COWARD or CUT AND RUN."

And the last line of the letter simply said, "I enclosed a photo of Pat Tillman, you probably know his story. Look in his eyes, and if you listen closely, you'll hear what he's calling you—a fraud."

I never responded, but I kept that letter for years. I couldn't bring myself to throw it away, even though I never responded. It haunted me. Not because it exposed something new, but because it confirmed something I had long feared to be true. Those words didn't create the shame I felt, but they found it.

That letter didn't just sting; it lodged itself inside me. Football had always been about chasing a childhood dream, but underneath that was a deeper motivator: the fear that I was never enough. And while this letter didn't create that fear, it amplified it. I ended up tying my identity even more closely to what I could produce. Every practice, every rep, and every ounce of sweat became part of the evidence I was gathering to prove that I wasn't a fraud.

To others, it may have looked like commitment and

discipline, but on the inside, it was something else entirely. It was the desperation of a man trying to outrun a story he didn't know how to put down. I worked harder, sacrificed more, and built a life around proving that I could carry the weight others doubted I could.

The thing about shame is that it rarely begins in the moments we feel it most intensely. Most of the time, it's already living inside us, waiting for something to confirm it. That letter didn't create the shame I carried, but it gave it fuel. And once shame has fuel, it can drive you harder than almost anything else. For me, that letter became proof of what I had feared all along, and from that point forward, my hustle tightened its grip.

Maybe you've experienced something like that too. A sharp word hurled your way, an impossible expectation, or a moment that stripped you bare. It didn't create shame; it merely confirmed it. And ever since, your drive hasn't only been about achievement, but about trying to outrun your fear and shame in an attempt to protect yourself from being seen as not enough.

The unfortunate reality is that no level of success can ever erase that kind of shame. If anything, it makes it grow stronger. The more you strive to escape it, the stronger it becomes.

Doubling Down Instead of Slowing Down

By the time my story had reached national headlines, discussions about my future were already taking place behind closed doors at the Department of Defense, among powerful people who'd never met me. However, none of those conversations ever involved me or made their way to me, my agent, or the Detroit Lions, who had just drafted me. We were all left in the dark.

On the morning that I was scheduled to sign my first NFL contract and report to my very first training camp, I got a call from my agent. His voice was serious and straight to the point as he told me to get to the stadium immediately. I wasn't supposed to be there for another few hours, so I knew something was wrong. When I arrived, I was ushered upstairs to a team meeting room full of every decision maker in the Lions organization. And pressure—loads of pressure. Something wasn't right.

With no warning, a government official from the Department of Defense coldly informed the room that two weeks earlier, the Pentagon had rescinded the policy that would have allowed me to play in the NFL while serving in the Army. The same policy I had trusted my future to since my sophomore year at West Point, and the same policy the Detroit Lions had trusted enough to use a draft pick on a West Point football player. And just like that, with the contract on the table next to me and my jersey hanging in the locker room downstairs, my dream was abruptly over.

I should have been devastated. Instead, I exhaled.

The shame and fear I was carrying had become so heavy that the pressure to perform under it was unbearable. Being told I couldn't play felt like a get-out-of-jail-free card. No public failure, no exposure, and no moment where the world could confirm my fear that maybe I really wasn't enough.

But instead of seeing that moment as a wake-up call, I saw it as a challenge. Instead of surrendering to the deeper invitation of inner growth being extended to me, one that might've asked me to slow down, feel, and be more present with my inner discomfort, I decided it was an opportunity for me to double down. So, I went back to the only strategies I knew: working harder, getting stronger, and earning it all back. If I could do that, I could outrun the turmoil inside me. My hope was that I could bury the shame and fear of being exposed under more muscle and more discipline.

So, I went back to the United States Army, and I did what was required of me. My days started before sunrise with physical fitness sessions with my unit at 5 AM, followed by military classroom work and field training exercises that stretched late into the afternoon. When everyone would go home after a long day of work, I would make my way back to the gym to put in the work needed to keep my childhood dream alive. For two and a half years, I lived this way. Soldier by day, NFL hopeful by night. Training in borrowed time, carrying a dream that most people had already moved on from. Most players don't come back after a season fully away. Almost none come back after more than two years—especially without being on a team, without reps, without film sessions, and without any momentum. I knew the odds, but I trained anyway.

As a result, I stayed in the kind of shape most people only dream of. I poured everything I had into becoming the best version of myself physically. Ultimately, it proved to be worthwhile. Against all expectations and after serving our country, I got a call and was invited to try out as a free agent. And when it was over, I was offered a new contract on the spot. After two years of service and a long absence from the game, I was back in the NFL.

But there was just one problem.

While I looked the part, I felt utterly fractured. The fear of exposure didn't go away; it intensified. I had everything I thought I needed to feel confident—my strength, my size, my speed, and now, my second chance—but nothing in me felt settled. What was once a whisper of insecurity had now grown to a full-sized roar. And the more I tried to silence it with effort, the louder it became.

Although I had worked hard to achieve the best shape of my life, it was evident that no amount of external effort or physical strength could address the inner struggle I was still facing.

I had grown up in worlds where vulnerability wasn't safe: evangelical Christianity, football team locker rooms, the military, the culture of masculinity I inherited. In those spaces, stillness was seen as laziness. Emotion was equated with weakness. And letting people see you struggle was dangerous. I didn't just avoid slowing down; I honestly didn't know it was allowed.

So, when my discomfort with my life started to spill over, I did what a lot of us do—I found ways to contain it by building walls around it. And when the pressure behind those walls got too heavy to hold, I started looking for ways to escape. That's what led me to nights out with strangers, to cocaine tucked into my bag, to parties that lasted until the sun came up. Then I'd drag myself to practice, smile, and pretend everything was fine.

And eventually, that fateful morning came.

I rolled over and saw the table next to my bed—the same image I opened this book with—and I knew. If something didn't change, I wouldn't survive this. That morning, I felt a lot of things—mainly shame and a headache from the night before. But somehow, in the midst of the brokenness, I had one of the most honest moments of my life. I decided to stop running. I stopped running toward the idea of what I thought my life was supposed to look like. And, most importantly, I stopped running away from the shame and pain the little boy in me had been carrying since childhood.

At the time, this decision didn't feel like it took courage as much as it felt like evidence of my failure and ultimate weakness. My entire life, I had been the strong one, the one who could always carry more, do more, take the hit, and keep going. But that strength that once helped me survive had unknowingly become my cage. After years of hustling, I had finally realized that my greatest fear—slowing down and being exposed—was exactly what I needed most.

Hustle may be our hiding place, but stillness is where we truly heal.

Healing in the Stillness

When I finally walked away from the NFL, I didn't step into a life of clarity, but one of stillness. The lights were off. The cameras were gone. The external pressure to achieve and the endless personal need to perform to secure my seat at the table were no longer necessary. What remained was just me—alone with the pain and shame I had spent years trying to outrun.

Through a strange series of events, none of which I could have scripted, I ended up moving to Canada. I didn't go for a job or an opportunity. I went because of a series of tweets from a church.

Their account kept discussing the idea that there is no new life without death. If you want to step into something new, you have to let go of the old. Growing up in church, I'd heard that before (usually around Easter), but this time it landed differently. I felt like I was dying, and there was nothing I wanted more than a new life.

The only problem was that letting go wasn't in my vocabulary. My whole life, I had been committed to doubling down, trying harder, and pushing through every challenge. But something in me recognized the wisdom in this teaching. So, I packed my bags and drove to Canada.

When I arrived there, I walked into that church and knocked on the pastor's door. I don't remember exactly what I said, but after fumbling through my words and telling him way too much of my story, I asked with tears in my eyes, "Can you help me?" Thankfully, without even knowing me, he said yes.

Over the next five years, I cleaned bathrooms, vacuumed floors, and changed lightbulbs in exchange for free therapy. My days were unimpressive by most standards, but for the first time in my life, I wasn't climbing any ladder or chasing any goal. I wasn't proving anything to anyone, other than myself. And surprisingly, I was happier than I had been in years.

Removing myself from the noise of my familiar life disrupted my patterns of self-sabotage, and I began to connect with the power of stillness. Within that stillness, there was the space to breathe, to notice what I couldn't see in the chaos, to feel what I had been too busy to feel, and to hear what my life had been trying to tell me.

The truth is, it's not the pace of life that wears us down. It's the pretense, the relentless posturing, proving, and performing that distances us from our true selves. That's what truly drains us. And the longer we resist stillness, the more energy we expend holding it all together—until the act of holding it together is the very thing that breaks us apart.

That's why stillness matters to our ability to thrive. It provides the necessary breathing room for the thoughts you've been avoiding, the grief you've been carrying, and the truth you've been sidelining and ignoring. Without it, you can live years—decades even—on autopilot, mistaking forward movement for progress.

You don't have to quit your job or move to another city to find stillness. External changes help, but they won't be enough because they don't create stillness—they only create the conditions for it. Stillness isn't about location. It's about ending the cycle of avoidance disguised as hustle and productivity. It's choosing to stop running long enough for the truth you've been avoiding to finally surface, even for a moment.

For me, I noticed the opportunity to practice stillness in the smallest, most ordinary places. I noticed it in the reflex to reach for my phone when I felt restless. The impulse to fill silence with something—anything. The pressure to stay productive, so I didn't have to sit with what was uncomfortable.

The work of stillness is simply to notice the impulse to avoid or distract and choose differently, to stay with the discomfort a few seconds longer than we want to, to let the sensation crest instead of rushing past it. These small moments of choosing stillness matter.

At first, stillness didn't feel peaceful—it felt unsettling.

Without the familiar distractions, the stories I had outrun for years rose to the surface. The fear of not being enough. The belief that my value depended on what I could produce. The shame I had buried beneath the never-ending forward motion.

Over time, what once chased me began to stand in front of me. And once it could be seen, it no longer needed to control me from the shadows. This is what stillness invites us into and where the deeper work begins. The work is no longer about *doing* more, but about staying present with what has been waiting beneath the surface. This is what stillness really is. Not an absence of activity, but an orientation of the heart. A way of relating to your inner world with openness instead of avoidance, with honesty instead of control. When we stop hiding in the hustle, we give the truth of our lives the space it needs to catch up to us. And when it does, something essential begins to shift.

Finding stillness doesn't mean everything around you slows down. Life will still race forward. The emails will still pile up. The kids will still need to be driven to practice. The deadlines won't disappear. But in the middle of it all, you'll find that you can begin to slow down inside. You can notice your breath. You can pause before reacting. You'll have the capacity to listen to what speaks in the stillness when you're not drowning it out with busyness.

Now is the time for the deeper work. No more hustling to prove ourselves or running from the parts of us we fear in the name of productivity. We must learn to live our lives from this posture. Not as an escape from our lives, but as a different way of entering them. Everything else builds from here.

A Gentle Invitation

As you move through the next week, pay attention to where your life naturally speeds up. Rushing out of the house. Moving quickly to pick up the kids. Jumping from one meeting to the next. Life will continue to demand speed at times, and that isn't the problem.

The problem is *how you move* when things move fast. See if you can notice the difference between rushing from a place of urgency and moving quickly from a place of presence. One feels tight and reactive. The other feels grounded and responsive. Even when life requires speed, there is a way to move from a posture of stillness.

Alongside this, notice the moments when you feel the urge to distract yourself or avoid certain feelings, when you reach for your phone or fill silence with noise. Notice when tinkering or *doing* becomes a way to avoid what you're feeling.

These moments are opportunities to practice stillness, and they add up.

Chapter Five

THE PAIN PARADOX

One day he told me that he'd spent his adulthood trying to let go of his past, and he remarked how ironic it was that he had to get closer to it in order to let it go.

—Bessel van der Kolk

Note to readers: This chapter includes a brief reference to suicide.

My sophomore year of football at West Point was a standout season. By the end of the season, I was not only among the top-rated safeties in college football, but my name was also beginning to appear in discussions about the NFL. That winter, I returned home for the holidays and unexpectedly found myself facing a TV camera for a regional news interview. In my hometown, this was the peak, and I felt a sense of pride at "making it."

To understand why that moment mattered so much, you first need to know where I come from. My hometown was the epitome of *Friday Night Lights,* where football wasn't just a sport—it was a religion. Fridays felt like sacred ground. The whole town gathered under the lights, watching to see if something holy would happen.

My childhood in that same hometown was anything but idyllic. I grew up in a strict religious environment where the rules were rigid, and expectations were even more immutable. With God on your side, failure wasn't even supposed to be part of the equation. My parents were deeply supportive, and they showed up in ways I'm still grateful for. At the same time, there was a fine line—one I didn't understand then—between their encouragement and something more complicated. Their pride in me was real, but so was the sense that my success carried meaning not just for me—but for all of us.

Being a "good Christian boy" only added to the weight I carried. I drew hard boundaries in my life, avoiding the more rebellious extracurricular activities that most high school students enjoyed. While others were experimenting with freedom and finding themselves, I stayed on the straight and narrow. And I paid the price for it. I was bullied, made fun of, and constantly left out of plans—everyone thought I acted like I was too good for them. I know it sounds silly, but words can cut, and these words cut deep.

The toll was so heavy that I found myself contemplating taking my own life more than once. The loneliness, the pressure, the feeling of never being enough all just became too much. Luckily, instead of breaking, I learned to channel the pain. I turned it into a fire, using it to fuel my ambition. *I'll prove them wrong; just watch and see,* quickly became my mantra. That pain and the need to prove my worth were the roaring engine driving me forward.

So, gaining recognition in the college football world while representing our country at West Point, and doing it all while publicly giving God the glory, was more than a big deal in my hometown. It was the ultimate trifecta, embodying everything the community valued most—faith, patriotism, and football.

The interview was supposed to be a feel-good segment—a chance for the town and local region to see a local boy on TV and for me to express gratitude for growing up in the Texas Panhandle. The questions were predictable: "What's it like playing at this level?" "How does it feel to make your hometown proud?" But then, the reporter threw me a curveball when he asked: "Do you think you'll ever come back home and coach here someday?"

I didn't even have to think about my answer because it flowed out of me effortlessly. It was almost like a part of me unknowingly wanted to be asked this question, and without even knowing it, I was ready. With an arrogant smile painted across my unabashed face, I said, "The only way I ever come back to live in this town is if I'm coming back to buy it."

The reporter laughed. The cameraman laughed. To them, it was a harmless joke. Cocky, sure, but still a joke. But I wasn't joking. I meant every word. And as their laughter trailed off, I held my gaze, letting them know I was dead serious.

In that moment, I believed the only way to silence my pain was to succeed so outrageously that no one could ever question my worth again. Success wasn't just a dream—it became my armor. Every accolade was proof that the words that once cut me couldn't define me. Every achievement was a shield against the loneliness I carried.

And underneath it all, the pain I had tried so hard to escape had become the fuel driving me forward.

Pain as Ambition

There's no denying that our past pain, whether rooted in childhood trauma or more recent wounds, can be a powerful motivator. It's a source of energy that fuels ambition and drives us to achieve. My own need to prove my critics wrong is far from a unique story. According to *Psychology Today*, this trauma is one of the most common forms of ambition, and for good reason—it works.

During my sophomore year at West Point, I was excelling as an athlete, but as a cadet, I was spiraling. I had just finished a breakout season that garnered the attention of NFL teams and agents. From the outside, it looked like everything was falling into place—especially since the Department of Defense had just implemented a new policy that would allow service academy graduates to pursue a professional sport and serve simultaneously, provided they received a professional contract.

At the same time, the pressure, fear, and pain I had been avoiding since I was a young boy were coming to the surface, and I didn't know what to do with them.

One morning, my body began to shut down from the inner distress I had been suppressing, and I had a complete meltdown. I ended up at sick call, trying to explain to the doctor what I couldn't even fully articulate to myself. I felt like I was losing my mind, and I had no idea what was happening. After a few minutes, she suggested I talk to a therapist.

I don't remember much about my first therapy session. I was numb and barely present, as the therapist asked questions and took notes. Toward the end of our conversation, he handed me a prescription and asked if I knew anything about depression. According to him, the medication would help with the heaviness I had carried for as long as I could remember.

Before I left, he asked if I had any questions. I only had one.

"Will the meds interfere with my anger?" He paused, clearly trying to make sense of what I was asking. I explained that my anger wasn't just an emotion—it was my edge, my fuel. I needed it. On the field, it was the fire that kept me going. Off the field, my anger was the way I regained control of any situation where I felt vulnerable or exposed. Without it, I was afraid I'd lose my edge, my drive. Without it, I worried I'd be left defenseless, exposed, and more susceptible to even greater pain.

He didn't have a definitive answer, but his hesitation was all I needed to decide. The space of hesitation between my question and his answer—though it lasted only a few seconds—was big enough for doubt to creep in, reminding me that I was on my own. By the time I returned to my room, my mind had been made up. I flushed the pills down the toilet. I didn't want anything to come between me and one of the primary weapons I used on the battlefield of life to ensure my survival and victory.

At the time, I didn't understand why I clung so tightly to my anger. It was all I knew. But years later, I realized why. My anger was easier to hold than pain, and if I let the anger go for even a moment, I would have to face the deeper wounds it was covering. That's when it clicked for me: My anger wasn't just a tool or a fire that kept me going. It was my shield, my armor, that I used to protect myself from the deeper wounds I wasn't ready to face—my pain.

Back in chapter one, I talked about how striving became my survival strategy—chasing the next win, the next goal, anything to prove I was enough. What I've come to see since then is that striving wasn't the whole story. It was just the outward expression of something deeper. Beneath it all was pain I didn't know how to face. And because I couldn't bear the pain, I turned it into anger—anger at being overlooked, underestimated, belittled, and dismissed. That anger became the thing telling me if I stopped proving myself, I'd be nothing. Striving was the way I moved through the world, anger was the fuel that kept me moving, and pain was the wound buried underneath it all.

My edge took the form of anger, but for some, it hides behind perfectionism or overwork. For others, it shows up as control, withdrawal, or people-pleasing. On the surface, these look like personality traits or habits. Underneath, they're all pain in disguise, pushing us to move through the world in ways that keep us from ever feeling our wounds directly.

Over time, those patterns don't just drive what we do—they shape who we believe we are. That's what I call *adaptations.*

Adaptations

When the ache is too much to face head-on, we bend ourselves around it. Over time, we become hardened into uncomfortable and unnatural shapes that feel permanent. These are our adaptations. They're influenced by our families, our communities, and the culture we grow up in. We learn what gets rewarded and what gets punished. We figure out how to stay safe, how to get love, how to belong. And often, without ever naming it, those adaptations start running our choices.

A child will intuitively learn that anger gets attention or that silence keeps the peace. A teenager will discover that achievement wins applause or that caretaking earns affection. Over time, what begins as a survival mechanism slowly calcifies into identity. Before long, we're not just acting a certain way—we believe this is who we are.

That's what happened to me. For years, I thought my edge, my fire, my relentless drive to prove myself was just my personality. But it wasn't my nature—it was my armor. An adaptation I had built so carefully and worn for so long that I couldn't imagine life without it.

The risk of adaptations lies not in their lack of usefulness. Rather, the risk is that they protect and serve us too effectively. They support us during times when we might not otherwise persevere. Although they start as a means of shielding us from pain, they ultimately bind us to it, persuading us that our armor defines who we are.

The moment that illusion cracks is the moment healing can begin. Because when the armor is no longer mistaken for the self, something hidden is revealed—the part of us that was being hidden by this protection all along.

That's when I finally met someone I had avoided for most of my life—my inner child.

Meeting the Inner Child

Most people don't think they have an inner child. They think they have a temper or anxiety, or they think they're just driven, guarded, hard on themselves, or bad at slowing down. What most of us miss is that these patterns didn't just come from nowhere.

Inner child work doesn't start with childhood memories. It starts in the moments when your reaction feels bigger than the situation in front of you—when a small disappointment stings like a deep rejection, or when approval feels necessary just to breathe, or when conflict feels threatening, even when the relationship isn't actually at risk.

That recognition is what eventually led me to this work and why it has been one of the most profound and transformative parts of my healing journey. At its heart, it's about reconnecting with the younger version of yourself—the child who learned to adapt in order to survive, but who also carries the wounds those adaptations were built around.

The inner child is more than a metaphor I encountered in a book; it genuinely exists as a living presence within each of us. It's the part that still remembers what it felt like to be left out, criticized, or unseen. It's the part that shows up as anger when we're really afraid, or as overachievement when we're desperate to be loved. Healing the inner child isn't about mending the past; rather, it's about allowing those parts of ourselves that never experienced safety, recognition, or love to finally receive that opportunity.

The little boy within me continued to manifest himself through expressions of anger, fear, and an unyielding desire to validate my worth. At first, the idea of meeting him felt strange—even embarrassing. But the deeper I went, the more I realized: This wasn't a gimmick. It was the most direct way to reach beneath the armor and connect with the part of me that had been longing for acknowledgment for decades.

When I moved to LA, I found myself in a city that exposed me in new ways, surfacing aspects of myself that I didn't know were still fractured. The newness of it all left me vulnerable, and I longed for connection and community. I somewhat naturally fell in with a Venice Beach crowd who were free-spirited but successful—the kind of people who knew how to float through life and reward themselves with a little extra on the weekends. Initially, finding these people and sharing life with them felt electric. *This is why people move to LA*, I thought to myself.

Growing up in the Texas Panhandle, especially in the evangelical culture, I was buried under rules. What to do and what not to do, what is sin and what is not sin. Now in LA, all the rules were gone, and I was completely unbridled. But slowly, the partying started to feel like self-betrayal, and I found myself repeating patterns that I thought I had already outgrown.

I came to LA with a sense of purpose, but I quickly began living in a way that didn't feel congruent with who I was. I had enough awareness at this time to realize that I was headed down a path that looked all too familiar, the same path that had almost taken my life only a handful of years earlier when I was burying the pain and pressure of being America's athlete in the NFL.

One afternoon in West Hollywood, the noise and

movement of the street became too much. My chest tightened. My vision blurred. My ears rang. I dropped to my knees, certain I was having a heart attack, but it was my biggest panic attack yet. I made it to a side street and collapsed against a tree, trying my best to ride it out.

By some miracle, the wave eventually passed, but I was left shaken and raw. Later that same afternoon, still trying to make sense of what had just happened, I mentioned it to a couple of people I knew in LA. Without hesitation, they told me I needed to see their Reiki healer.

I had heard of Reiki, but only vaguely. And even though I had grown and evolved beyond the evangelical Christianity I was raised in, there was a tiny part of me that still believed that anything that involved energy work sounded like something I should avoid, repent for, or at least call my mom about. But I was desperate, so I booked an appointment for later that afternoon.

Reiki, as I learned in the thirty minutes before my session, with my old religious wiring fully activated as I panic-googled "*is Reiki demonic*" on my phone, is a Japanese healing practice built on the idea that the body has its own energy system—something I had spent most of my life pretending didn't exist. Practitioners place their hands lightly on or above the body to work with that energy. At the time, it felt like a foreign language, but the panic attack had left me with very few options. I was willing to try anything.

For sixty minutes, I lay on a table while the practitioner did her thing. I can't tell you if the session helped, but what she said afterward did. She taught me about breathwork and told me how this tool had changed her life. Then she said, "My friend Rob is hosting a session tonight—you should go."

That night, I walked into Rob's breathwork class in Venice Beach. In the span of a single day, I'd gone from crumpling on the sidewalk in West Hollywood to lying on the floor of a dimly lit room with twenty strangers, about to meet a part of myself I'd been avoiding my entire life.

Rob greeted me at the door. He was short and bald, his neck adorned with three different layers of beads and a large crystal. And yet, what I noticed first wasn't his appearance but the way he radiated light. The kind of light you carry only when you've faced the darkest parts of your story and let them remake you. I felt it the moment I saw him.

As soon as we stepped inside, I teared up. For the first time in a long time, I felt the tangible presence of love wrap around me like a warm blanket on a cold night. I felt at home. Rob shared pieces of his story, how he had been homeless, addicted, and broken until he found his breath. Literally. He shared with us that as he breathed, something awakened in him. A language began to flow, and he started to sing in a tongue he'd never learned.

When he demonstrated it, I almost fell over. I knew that sound. He was speaking in tongues. Praying in tongues was a big deal in my childhood faith, as it was seen as evidence that the Holy Spirit was present and moving through you. Some received it; some didn't. Those who did, like me, carried an unspoken sense that something meaningful had happened. But here I was, in Venice Beach, hearing someone pray in tongues who didn't even believe in God.

Growing up, I was taught to believe Christianity was the ocean. But here, in this room, I began to see that love was the ocean and Christianity, like every other religion, was just a wave. Each of us was made of the same water but shaped in different ways. With every step on my healing journey, my understanding of God further collapsed.

Eventually, the session began. I lay on my back, breathing with twenty strangers. One breath, then another, then another. My breath found the rhythm of the music, and as the tempo built, so did the intensity in my body. Breathwork is wild—your face goes numb, your hands cramp, your body tingles like you've just taken a powerful psychedelic. But it's just your breath.

Halfway through, something in me locked up. I could feel the breath moving from my head, through my chest, down toward my belly, but it stopped just before my groin. There was a deep resistance. I didn't know what to do but keep going. I pushed the breath into the place that didn't want it, and suddenly something broke open. Emotion rushed in, and I began to weep—not cry, but weep—hysterically.

At the end, Rob led a meditation and asked us to return to our earliest happy memory. I scanned my past but came up empty. Every memory felt heavy. Before I could find one, panic crept in, and I feared I was about to lose the breakthrough I'd just experienced.

Rob must have sensed it. He came over, gently placed his hands on my shoulders, and grounded me. That's when it happened—an out-of-body experience. I saw myself, adult Caleb, floating above where I lay. And beneath me, I saw him—the little boy I used to be. Fragile, scared, and alone.

Almost immediately, adult me began to whisper, "It's not your fault. It's not your fault. It's not your fault." The words weren't just a mantra—they were a lifeline. With each repetition, I reached back through time to the boy who had been carrying responsibility for other people's emotions, the pressure to be strong at all times, the shame he couldn't name, and the belief that love and acceptance were always tied to performance.

I sobbed, not from my head, but from somewhere far deeper. A pain I didn't even know I was holding had finally been given permission to be felt and released.

In the middle of this moment, I felt a hand. The stranger next to me reached over and held mine. I can't remember how long he held my hand, but it offered me enough compassion and safety that I was able to stay present in the vulnerability of the moment.

When the music faded, and the lights came up, I sat there, exhausted and fully cracked open. I turned to the man beside me and said, "Thank you." We hugged, and as I pulled away, I caught his face in the light. It took me a second, but then it hit me. The man who had held my hand while I met my inner child was Andre 3000. Yes, that Andre 3000 from Outkast.

One minute, I was having a panic attack in West Hollywood. The next, I was breathing with a bald man wearing a crystal, speaking in tongues, meeting my inner child in an out-of-body experience, and being comforted by a '90s hip-hop icon.

Healing is wild. Healing in Los Angeles is wilder.

Our Wound Is Our Womb

That night on the floor of the breathwork house changed me. Not because I walked out with some perfect, cinematic closure or neat resolution to my pain. It was because, for the first time, I met the part of me who had been carrying it all along. I didn't try to fix him or tell him to toughen up. I didn't shame him for the ways he had learned to protect himself. I simply whispered the words he had always needed to hear: *It's not your fault.* Those four words felt like a lifeline thrown across decades of distance. I was finally bearing witness to him—seeing the little boy who had been hidden underneath the armor and adaptations—and letting his story out. Recognition is what always begins to set the wound free.

In reality, many of us dedicate our lives to alleviating our pain. We bury it beneath success, dull it with busyness, and mask it with perfection or control. But relief isn't the same as healing. Healing isn't about the absence of pain; rather, it's the ability to embrace it without being overwhelmed. You can feel it without letting it dictate your choices. When we allow ourselves to remain present with our pain, observing it with compassion rather than judgment, a transformation occurs. The wound may remain, but it no longer controls us. In that very space, the place that once brought only pain, new beginnings start to emerge.

The Greeks told a story that captures this truth. Chiron, the centaur, was abandoned at birth and carried rejection as his deepest wound. He searched everywhere for a cure. He mastered medicine, learned from the wisest teachers, and discovered remedies that could heal almost anyone. Almost, because no matter what he tried, he couldn't heal himself.

Over time, his relationship with his wound changed. He stopped seeing it as an enemy that he needed to defeat. He began to live with it—not in resignation, but in acceptance. And through that acceptance, something unexpected happened—his wound no longer consumed him. Instead, it became a source of wisdom. The very place he ached the most became the place from which he could truly help others.

Upon hearing Chiron's story for the first time, my healing journey started to become clearer. His wound never fully healed, but his relationship with it evolved. Healing didn't make him pain-free—it made him free. Free to love, free to serve, free to live without being defined by what hurt him the most. The paradox lies in the fact that our wounds may never completely heal, yet when we learn to hold them with compassion rather than resistance, they lose the power to shrink our lives. They can transform into the source that nurtures wisdom, love, and a renewed way of living.

This is the work we are being invited to engage with. You don't need to discover the ideal remedy or eliminate the pain entirely to begin living. However, you must prepare yourself for the process of healing. Preparing your heart isn't about bracing for impact; it's about developing the capacity to stay open when things feel uncomfortable, uncertain, or overwhelming. For you, that preparation may not begin with a significant moment on a breathwork floor. It may begin in the simplest and most everyday triggers, such as when you realize you don't actually know what to do next, when doubt creeps in and you feel exposed, or when you feel behind and full of fear. These are the moments that matter. When instead of reacting, fixing, or powering through, you pause and ask, *What's really happening here? What's the deeper invitation I'm being offered here?*

Little moments like these are how we begin building our capacity to hold pain instead of running from it. One of the most practical ways I know to do that is a framework I've taught to thousands of leaders as a keynote speaker—I call it the inner advantage.

The Inner Advantage

By the time most people reach a certain level in life, they've mastered the external game—setting goals, solving problems, pushing through hard days, producing results at any cost. But very few have learned how to work with the internal pressure that comes with it. They keep sprinting, thinking more effort will fix what they feel. In reality, the strain is happening inside of them, not around them.

That's why so many high-performing people eventually hit a wall that doesn't always look like burnout at first. It looks like irritability, a never-ending exhaustion, a loss of joy and purpose, or the fear that they don't have another gear left, and the way they're doing life is unsustainable. This isn't a performance issue. It's a capacity issue—the gap between the demands we face and our ability to hold those demands without collapsing under them.

And the world isn't slowing down.

So, the true advantage in life can't be the old advantage anymore. It's not the people who grind the hardest or outlast everyone in the room. The advantage now belongs to those who know how to meet the pressure of high performance differently. Not by resisting it or numbing it, but by expanding within it.

That is the inner advantage. It's a method of confronting life's pressures and discomforts that transforms what once drained us into something that can help us grow. It's the practice of turning discomfort into capacity, fear into wisdom, and emotional weight into a groundedness that allows you to stay rooted and present when things get hard. The same fuel that once burned hot and dirty can be transformed into clean and steady energy to sustain the life we long to live.

The inner advantage works in a simple rhythm that I refer to as the three R's: recognize, reframe, respond.

Recognize—The first step is noticing the moment when something inside you flares up or tightens. It's the moment when you find yourself wanting to shut down from insecurity, or the impulse to prove yourself out of the fear of being overlooked, or jumping into overthinking and perfectionism because managing every detail feels easier than sitting with what's really going on inside of you. The moment you can name these reactions for what they are—old survival patterns kicking in—you interrupt the surface-level autopilot that's blinding you to your true inner landscape. Recognition creates a pause, and within that pause is the power to make a different choice. We can't get to something new without first becoming someone new, and this is where it starts.

Reframe—None of us gets through a day without feeling some level of stress, tension, or discomfort. It's part of the human experience. But almost no one meets those moments with excitement. We don't throw our hands in the air and say, "Yes! This is growth—I'm expanding." More often, we read discomfort as a problem. From our families, our culture, and sometimes our faith traditions, many of us learned to see the edges of our capacity as evidence of inadequacy. So, when pain or discomfort surfaces, it's tempting to push through it or try to just make it disappear. These edges mark the places where growth is possible if we learn how to befriend what's emerging rather than resist it. Reframing is about choosing to see the moment you're in not as a threat, but as an opening. So, instead of rushing to worst-case scenarios when tension bubbles up, ask, *What does facing this make possible?* That question turns the very thing you once feared into the entry point for your next stage of growth.

Respond—Once you recognize the signal and shift the meaning of it, the next step is responding in a way that restores safety inside of you. These signals show up because somewhere in your system, something feels unsafe or threatened—even if the situation isn't dangerous. Responding isn't about fixing the moment or trying to be strong. It's about taking one small, tolerable step that helps your body regulate. That step might be a slower breath, feeling your feet on the floor, naming what's happening inside of you, or taking a walk and practicing presence. Because each time you choose presence over pattern, you send a signal to your autonomic nervous system and show your body that you're okay right now. Over time, those small moments of safety start to rewrite the story you live from, expanding your tolerance and changing the way you move through moments that used to overwhelm you—reshaping how you move through the world.

Small, consistent steps in this rhythm create surprising momentum over time. You don't need a big breakthrough to begin your healing. You just need the willingness to face what's happening inside you, the courage to stay with it a little longer than you used to, and the patience to give the process time to work.

This framework is what shifted everything for me. And it can do the same for you.

The anger that once kept me alive no longer runs my life. I don't need it to feel safe anymore. It still visits sometimes, but now I can recognize it as an old adaptation trying its best to protect me and then choose a different response.

The pain that once fueled me (and crippled me) no longer has control of me. By learning to hold it and witness it, I turned it from a burden to an opportunity and opened up a way to live as the person I was always becoming. I don't need to buy a town to prove I belong anymore. I know now that the road back to myself is the only ground I need to own.

A Gentle Invitation

When I began my own healing work, I knew I had to learn how to interrupt my automatic reactions to moments of discomfort. The familiar ways I responded—pushing harder, numbing out, staying busy—kept me locked in survival and kept my life small. For an entire year, I carried a small notebook in my back pocket. Every time I felt discomfort surface in my everyday life, I stopped what I was doing and wrote it down. That was it.

Over time, this simple practice created space between what was happening within me and my response to it. And in that space, I began to choose differently. Slowly, the patterns that had once run my life loosened their grip. I didn't eliminate discomfort, but I stopped being run by it.

For the next few days, begin paying attention to the signals of your life. Each time you feel discomfort surface—tension, irritation, doubt, anxiety—pause and write it down. You can use a small notebook or the notes app on your phone. Don't analyze it or try to fix it. Just notice it and name it.

This practice isn't about tracking your flaws. It's about building awareness. When you start noticing these moments and naming them, they lose some of their power over you. What once ran your life from the background begins to come into view.

Chapter Six

PULLING THE CORD

One of the best kept secrets in life is that when you think you're falling into the void, you're really returning to yourself. What you think is going to be empty is actually full.

— *Penny Pierce*

Toward the end of my football career, my life felt like it was on the verge of imploding every single day. The tension inside me had become unbearable. Not the kind of tension that motivates you, but the kind that robs you of your sleep and makes the day feel heavy before it's even begun.

I was starving for connection, but the cracks in my perfectly crafted facade were beginning to show. I was surrounded by people, living the life I had always imagined, and yet I had never felt lonelier. So, when a group of teammates invited me to a theme park on our day off, I said yes without hesitation . . . even though I loathed theme parks.

My dislike went back to a childhood moment I could still feel in my bones.

I was maybe eight years old, visiting family in Colorado Springs, when I ended up on a carnival roller coaster. The ride operator strapped me in, or so I thought, and we took off. It wasn't until we were suspended high in the air, hanging upside down, that I realized my harness wasn't secure and I had started to slide out.

I immediately began to panic as my small hands gripped the safety bar that wasn't keeping me safe. My dad, seated next to me, reached over and hooked his arm around me, holding me in place while yelling at the ride operator. I don't remember how long we stayed suspended like that, but I will never forget the terror of sliding out of that seat, completely at the mercy of someone else's awareness.

Even as I grew older, the fear I experienced that day stayed lodged in my body. Theme parks weren't about rides or cotton candy. They were always about the boy inside me who was still afraid of falling, afraid of not being held.

But at this stage of my life in the NFL, my desperation for connection outweighed my fear. So, I went. We spent the day moving through the park, my teammates buzzing with energy. I became skilled at dodging rides that made my palms sweat by taking a well-timed phone call, offering to buy the next round of beers, or making a sudden detour to the restroom.

I thought I was home free as we were steps from the exit when one of my teammates stopped and said, "Guys, we have to do this." Looking to my left, my teammate, Zeke, was pointing to a towering ride where two people were strapped into a harness, hoisted hundreds of feet into the air, and then dropped into a free fall. Hell no. My stomach sank. I searched for an excuse, but the math was against me. There were six of us, which meant if I bailed, someone would ride with a stranger. I couldn't be that guy.

Minutes later, I was dangling high above Kansas City, strapped into the harness, staring at what looked like a repurposed traffic-light signal. When the light went from red to yellow to green, it would be my job to pull the cord and release us. When the moment came and the light turned green, I froze. My hands were glued to the cord. My arms felt heavy, my shoulders locked. My heartbeat pounded in my ears.

Zeke, strapped beside me, hysterically laughing, started yelling for me to pull the cord. After a few shouts, his tone shifted. He could tell I wasn't just hesitating—I was panicking. Immediately, his voice softened. He started speaking to me like a compassionate friend, not a motivational teammate, and his calm demeanor somehow lessened the intensity of the roar of fear rising within me. After a few minutes, which felt like hours, I found enough courage to act, and I pulled the cord.

The first fraction of a second in the free fall was pure terror.

Every muscle in my body tensed as I braced for impact. But then, something unexpected happened. As gravity continued to pull us to the ground, the fear gave way to freedom. My body stopped resisting, and seemingly out of nowhere, I started laughing—the deep, uncontrollable kind that feels like it's coming from deep within your belly. Before I knew it, tears streamed down my face.

For maybe the first time in my life, I felt alive—really alive.

At the time, I thought this moment was about conquering a childhood fear, and it felt good. But years later, I would see it for what it really was: a foreshadowing. This wasn't just a theme park ride. It was a living metaphor for the life I was being invited to live. For the first time, I experienced what it was like to let go—to stop clinging to the illusion of control and trust that something bigger was holding me.

Up until that point, my life had been held together by sheer willpower and ruthless determination. I had chased the external edge and chased it well. But I was exhausted. That day gave me a taste of a different way of being—one that didn't depend on my endless effort to hold it all together.

And I wanted more.

Our Original Knowing

In his book *Mindful Cognitive Behavioral Therapy*, Seth J. Gillihan tells the story of red-tailed hawks who travel thousands of miles as they migrate from the United States and Canada to Mexico and Central America, averaging about seventy miles per day. These long trips are made possible only by their ability to find and ride thermals—invisible updrafts of warm air that can carry them for miles with little to no effort.

Scientists understand that hawks identify thermals by using their keen eyesight, sensing slight variations in air currents with their wings, and observing the circling patterns of other birds. However, finding the thermal is not sufficient, regardless of how they locate it. To be carried, they must stop flapping.

When I read that, I knew it wasn't just about hawks. It was about us. We spend so much of our lives flapping—overworking to prove we belong, trying to control outcomes so we feel safe, forcing relationships or roles that have already run their course, or staying in constant motion because stillness feels like danger. Flapping is how we learned to survive.

Survival isn't the same as being carried.

Hawks reveal that life has currents designed to propel us further than we could ever go alone. To truly experience that, we must release our constant striving and let the unseen lift us. We must abandon the frantic motion we've been conditioned to depend on. And if you've built your whole life on flapping, the stillness of being carried can feel like falling—and failing.

But it's not just that—it's a form of remembering.

From the very beginning, we were held. Long before we could speak or prove anything, something outside of us was sustaining our lives. In the womb, we were surrounded, nourished, and protected without having to earn it. Many of the ancient wisdom traditions point to this as our *original knowing*—a deep, felt sense of belonging and safety that lives in the body. While we may not consciously remember this belonging, our bodies do.

But eventually, life teaches us a different lesson. We fall, and no one's there to pick us up. We cry, and comfort doesn't always come. The world doesn't hold us the way we were once held, and so we learn to adapt. We learn to reach for the things that keep us safe. In the beginning, we reach for a stuffed animal or a special blanket. As adults, we reach for relationships, promotions, achievements, or addictions—anything that helps us feel safe and held.

Eventually, I realized that my endless striving wasn't about success—it was about trying to arrive at a version of life where I finally felt held. Success became something it was never meant to be—a survival strategy. I needed the next win, the next opportunity, the next "You're doing great" to lessen the panic that was lightly restrained inside me. I looked to success to offer the comfort and certainty I didn't know how to give myself. But no amount of success could do that. External achievement can't offer lasting internal stability. And when I finally learned that lesson, everything changed.

Instead of pouring all my energy into chasing the next milestone, I began learning what it meant to create safety within myself (more on this in chapter eight). I practiced regulating rather than reaching. I learned to slow down rather than speed up. I learned to hold myself in ways I had once expected the world to do for me. This raised a new question: If being held doesn't come from achievement, where does it come from?

To be held, we must first let ourselves fall.

The Wisdom of Surrender

As someone who spends most of my time speaking to leaders and organizations about leadership, inner growth, success, and well-being, I've learned that there are words you have to dance around in corporate spaces. *Surrender* is one of them. It can sound like defeat. It can signal weakness. In a world where we reward people for holding on tighter, pushing longer, and forcing outcomes, surrender can feel like the opposite of progress.

Part of the reason it feels so threatening is because many of us have built our identity on striving. We learned to stay safe by staying in control, by anticipating every possibility, by outworking whatever scared us. So when we hear the word *surrender*, it doesn't just challenge our habits—it challenges the very self we've relied on to survive. That's why surrender can feel like a kind of death. It asks us to let go of the version of ourselves that only knew how to move through life by gripping tighter. But there comes a point when moving life forward no longer happens through trying harder. It happens through resisting less.

The truth is, the very thing we avoid is often the thing

we most need. When most of us hear the word *surrender*, we imagine ourselves waving the white flag, abandoning the fight, or letting life roll over us. No wonder it feels like weakness. But that's not true surrender. It's not giving up—it's giving over. Giving over begins when we resist less, when we stop white-knuckling life, and when we allow ourselves to be carried by it.

Giving up is what happens when something inside you shuts down. You stop caring about the outcome, not because it doesn't matter to you, but because staying engaged feels too heavy. You disconnect so you don't have to feel the disappointment or fear. You lose energy or interest because you're overwhelmed. It's collapse—a protective response that steps in when you don't believe things can change. Giving over is different. You're still in it, and you still care. You're still showing up, but you stop trying to force what you can't control. You loosen your grip without losing your commitment. You let the moment be what it is instead of trying to muscle it into what you think it should be. Giving over begins when you resist less, when you stop gripping life so tightly and allow yourself to be carried by it in ways you can't engineer.

Giving over isn't disengagement. Rather, it's engagement without the fear-driven grip. It's a shift from fighting against life to participating in it.

When you surrender, you open space for the unseen to manifest. You enable unexpected possibilities to emerge. You cease insisting that the outcome unfold according to your terms and timeline, thereby creating space for the life you are truly meant to live, rather than merely the one you have been attempting to force into existence.

I have watched what happens when people can't make this shift. They hold on to the strategies, identities, and roles that once brought them success long after those ways of being have stopped serving them. They continue to flap their wings by doubling down on effort instead of seeking the current that will support their journey. What follows is predictable—burnout, stagnation, and a gradual loss of motivation and overall life satisfaction.

I've also observed what happens when people do surrender. They recognize that what got them here won't get them there. They cease attempting to impose the season they desire and begin to embrace the season they are truly experiencing. They accept endings as final, thereby creating room for genuine beginnings to emerge.

This wisdom is represented everywhere in nature. Look closely, and you'll see that nothing in nature resists its own letting go. When a tree sheds its leaves, it's not failing—it's conserving energy for the next season. When a snake outgrows its skin, the old layer doesn't cling on—it releases so the new one can form. Even the tide pulls back so it can return with force. There is no panic in nature when the season turns. Nothing tries to hold on to what has already served its purpose. Letting go is nature's way of making room for what's next.

And yet, we humans are persistently the one part of creation that refuses to do this. Instead of meeting what's happening with an open and curious heart, we tense up. We fight the falling. We try to outthink the moment, bargain with it, or push it back into something familiar. We try to hold on to seasons that have already ended, convincing ourselves that with enough effort, we can keep them alive. We refuse to give over to the natural cycle of death and rebirth, and in doing so, we resist the inner growth we need the most.

Giving over—the willingness to surrender—is not passive. It's the courage to live without guarantees, to stop tying your self-worth to outcomes and keep faith in a process that you cannot fully control. It's the choice to loosen your grip on life and face your fears. When you do, you'll discover an entirely new type of hope—one that doesn't rise and fall with your circumstances.

A Hope That Holds

Most of us were introduced to the concept of hope from an early age, as soon as we could comprehend language. For some, it came through religion. Maybe, like me, you were told to have hope that God would answer your prayers, open the right doors, and fix what was broken. That hope was always linked to results: healing, breakthroughs, or new paths. When life unfolded as planned, it felt powerful. However, when the doors remained closed, when the prayer went unanswered, and when the breakthrough never materialized, that hope began to unravel. No one instructed us on how to handle hope when the outcome did not meet our expectations.

Others built their sense of hope on the back of effort. We were told to hope for a better future by working harder, staying ahead, and hustling more. This is a hope that promises *If you just keep grinding, one day you'll arrive.* But no matter how much we achieve, there comes a point when the next win doesn't deliver what we thought it would. When our efforts don't produce the anticipated outcome, that hope collapses too.

And then there's the hope we place in ourselves—*if I just stay disciplined enough, strong enough, smart enough, I'll be okay.* For a while, it works. But eventually, no matter how tough or talented we are, we hit a wall we can't push past. And when our self-sufficiency fails, that form of hope breaks just like the others.

The problem with all these versions—religious, cultural, even self-reliant—is that they are conditional. They hinge on the outcome matching the expectation, whether it's God answering our prayer, the hustle paying off, or our own strength always being enough. If the outcome comes through, we feel hopeful. If it doesn't, the bottom falls out.

The distinction lies between the hope we are given and the hope we find for ourselves. A hope we have been given doesn't hold because it relies on the promises or systems of others. We discover hope for ourselves by creating our own history with life, and it holds. Whenever we relax our grip and embrace the wisdom of surrender, we feel in our bodies that we are still being supported. Such lived experiences foster a hope that no book, course, sermon, or mantra can provide. Only life itself can.

This newfound hope is not dependent on results. It doesn't require circumstances to line up before you feel steady. It resides within your body. It's the deep strength that rises when everything familiar falls away, and yet you are still here. It's what remains when the prayer isn't answered in the way you hoped, when the deal falls through, when the job is lost, when the relationship ends. It's the presence that softly reassures you: *You are still being supported.*

This kind of hope cannot be produced through positive thinking or motivational speeches. You cannot achieve it through mantras or sheer willpower. It can be gained only through lived experience and by embracing the act of letting go in those moments when you doubt your ability to endure, only to realize that the current is still supporting you.

When you start to live from this deeper sense of hope, it transforms everything. You stop treating uncertainty as the enemy. You cease to evaluate stability based on the predictability of your life. You navigate the unknown with a steadiness that remains unaffected by your circumstances.

That steadiness changes how you move through your life. You stop overpreparing for conversations that haven't happened yet. You stop postponing decisions until certainty arrives. You stop clinging to situations that are already asking to be released. Failure still hurts, but it no longer defines you.

And from this place, a different kind of confidence is born.

Before I reached the NFL, all my confidence came from my talent. I was faster, stronger, and more disciplined than most of the people I played with. On my best days, that confidence felt limitless—until I walked into the NFL and realized that everyone else was just as talented, if not more, than me. Suddenly, what had once made me sure of myself was no longer enough. Every missed tackle, every mistake in practice chipped away at the confidence I had built on being "the best."

When your confidence is built only on what you can do, it's always one failure away from collapsing.

However, the confidence that emerges from a steadfast hope is distinctly different. It doesn't rise and fall with performance. It remains present even when you are outmatched or overwhelmed. It's the kind of confidence that says, *Even if I fail, even if I don't measure up, I will still be held.*

That alters how you navigate through life. You cease to make decisions driven by the fear of failure. You begin to embrace the risks you've been evading because you are no longer relying solely on your ability to dictate the outcome. Most importantly, you can exchange the fear and worry about what may or may not occur for the joy that is present today.

Think about it. What would you try? What risk would you take? What leap would you finally make, if you knew you were always being held? Because that's what this kind of hope gives you—not just the ability to endure, but the freedom to step boldly into places that once terrified you.

This is the significance of surrender. This is why letting go matters. Only in free fall can you discover the type of hope that sustains. The kind of hope that has the power to carry you through your unstriving journey and the rest of your life. The kind of hope that endures when every other version falters.

In our home, we say those two words often: *We're held.*

We say them when money slows, when community fractures, when uncertainty presses in. They're not just words we've read somewhere. They represent the truth of our experiences. Every time we've pulled the cord in our own lives, we've landed on those words. Although circumstances may feel uncertain and unfamiliar, the current has never ceased to flow, and it has always held us steady.

This is the invitation of surrender: to trade control for trust. To pull the cord and find, in the free fall, a hope that holds.

When I let go of the NFL, it felt like a loss. And it was. But it also made room for a life I could never have imagined—a life better in ways my striving self would have never thought to dream of. I'm guessing the same is true for you.

Giving over doesn't happen in one big leap. It happens through a thousand small choices—choosing to loosen your grip, choosing to stop clinging to the way things used to be, choosing to trust the current you cannot control. Every choice carries risk, yet together they can make way for a life of safety and hope.

You simply have to pull the cord.

A Gentle Invitation

If you're wondering where to start, don't overcomplicate it. Identify just one area of your life right now where you've been white-knuckling an outcome, or where you've been forcing, managing, or controlling to the point of exhaustion.

If you want to practice surrender, start by noticing what fear shows up when you think about letting go of whatever it is you're white-knuckling. Is it the fear of failure, of being unseen, of losing control, of being alone? Write it down. Naming the fear breaks its power over you. Plus, you can't give up something you refuse to name.

Now, think back to a moment when life closed a door you desperately wanted to stay open. Something ended, fell apart, or didn't go the way you hoped. Now, ask a different question—not *why did this happen?*, but *what grew because it did?*

Maybe you learned you could trust yourself without external validation. Maybe you discovered a strength you didn't know you had. Maybe you realized you were okay being alone. Maybe you found a capacity, a clarity, or a courage that never would have emerged otherwise.

Acknowledge these moments and write them down. In a few sentences, write what evolved in you or around you because life *didn't* cooperate.

This becomes your *What Grew List*—a reminder that you're always being held.

Because when you find yourself at this threshold again—when life is asking you to pull the cord, and fear insists you won't survive the fall—you will need proof.

Return to your *What Grew List* and let it remind you that every time what you wanted fell through the cracks, something else grew in its place. This knowing is what supports you in loosening your grip and stepping forward once more—not because you're certain of the outcome, but because experience has taught you that you are always being held.

Chapter Seven

TRUSTING THE DISAPPEARANCE

I have faith in the night.

—Rainer Maria Rilke

Nothing could have prepared me for my first experience of Los Angeles. Around the time of that visit, I had started to post publicly about my journey from West Point to the NFL and the healing journey I had been on since walking away. A company in LA had reached out after reading my story online and invited me to visit so we could explore collaborating on a potential project together. We met, we talked, we had a great time, but ultimately, we realized there was nothing there.

A few hours before my flight home, I took a sunrise walk along Venice Beach. The boardwalk was mostly empty, the air was still cool, and the sound of the waves reminded me of the noise machine I used to fall asleep at night. As I walked along the boardwalk, I started to feel this trip to LA wasn't about a potential collaboration. This trip was the universe's way of getting me to LA so I could see that it would be my next home.

Canada had been my home for several years. It was where I first learned stillness and, more importantly, where I learned to tell the truth about what was really happening in my life. That season healed me in deep and profound ways, but I couldn't ignore the sense that something was beginning to shift. The clarity I had found there had begun to blur. The space that once felt expansive now felt tight. The very routines that had helped me uncover the truth about my life had grown heavy. Each day I stayed there began to feel like a slow betrayal of the truth I had worked so hard to uncover.

It was becoming increasingly clear to me that the same inner knowing that once pulled me away from football and toward Canada was stirring again, but this time it was pulling me somewhere new entirely. I didn't understand what it meant or where it was pointing, only that I was living inside a tension I could no longer ignore.

Los Angeles had never been on my radar. In my mind, it

was a city for dreamers and creatives, not for someone like me: a recovering meathead from a small Texas town where I grew up walking pigs. At the time, I was still trying to figure out my life. Moving there felt about as realistic as moving to Mars.

Yet that morning, with the sun breaking over the Santa Monica Mountains, I knew what was being asked of me. Once again, it was time to let go of what was familiar and choose the unknown. It was time to move to Los Angeles.

The City of Angels . . . and Unmet Expectations

It doesn't take long after arriving in Los Angeles to feel the buzz of the city. Possibility is everywhere, and before long, you start to believe anything could happen. For me, it felt like the universe was giving me a nod of approval, like it was saying, *This is what happens when you follow your heart.*

After leaving the NFL, choosing stillness over striving, and spending years in the hidden work of healing, I thought this was where it would all come together. The brand deals, the book, the speaking career—all of it would finally take shape. I thought this was where all the letting go would begin to make sense.

But the longer I was there, the more that picture began to blur. The city that first felt like pure possibility turned into a string of false starts: meetings that went nowhere, promises that evaporated, opportunities that got close enough for me to taste, then slipped away. Each one carried the hope of arrival, only to dissolve into another almost.

It reminded me of a game I used to waste money on at the arcade. You guide the claw over the prize, drop it down, and grab the prize. For a moment, you're sure you've won. But halfway to the chute, the prize inevitably slips through the arms. Without even thinking, you reach back into your pocket for more quarters, convinced the next time will be different, even though it never is. The game is designed that way. That's how false starts work in life. They feel like progress without ever being progress. They keep you hopeful enough to stay in the game. In its own way, life in LA started to feel this way.

We all do this in our own ways. The move across the country that we believe will finally open our life up. The next relationship that we're certain is going to be different this time around. The deal, promotion, or launch is finally going to deliver what we're searching for. We carry around a picture in our heads of how life is supposed to look. At first, when the picture doesn't match reality, it's frustrating but not crushing. We shove our hands deep into the metaphorical pockets of life and pull out more motivation and ambition and tell ourselves to push harder and try again. So, we double down on expectation instead of examining it. We keep living one step ahead of life, and over time, the gap of unmet expectations begins to wear us down as we make a home in the space between what we imagined and what is.

That was my life in LA. Another meeting, another

introduction, another open door. Each time, I told myself this was the one—the thing that would change everything. But the prize I was chasing, the life I wanted, kept slipping away. And like the arcade, I kept digging deeper, pulling out more ambition, more willpower, and trying again. But the goalposts were always moving ten yards further down the field.

Thankfully, not everything in LA was disappointing. It's where I met Kara, the best thing that ever happened to me. But even with that gift, so much of what I thought this season would be was slowly disappearing. After enough rounds with life, it wasn't just my body that felt worn down—it was my soul.

The most challenging aspect of a false start isn't merely the missed opportunity. It's witnessing the story you've crafted in your mind gradually fade away. You didn't just want the outcome—you built your hope on it. You imagined who you would become once it worked. And each time it didn't, you were left carrying the weight of a life that never arrived.

That's what LA became for me—a string of almosts. Doors that opened but didn't lead anywhere. Promises that gradually vanished into silence. I told myself to stay hopeful, keep my head up, and stay open, but underneath, a heaviness was forming—a slow, deep grief for a life that wasn't unfolding the way I thought it would. I tried to fight it, to summon that old "do more, be more" energy that had carried me through other hard seasons, but it just wouldn't come.

And just when I believed the weight couldn't become any heavier, the world came to a halt.

Trust the Heaviness of Life

When COVID hit, everything stopped. My work, my rhythm, and my community were gone overnight. Like so many others, I tried to pivot, but whatever momentum I had remaining slipped through my fingers. The uncertainty I felt in that time was bigger than my ability to carry it, and there was no fighting it.

One night, Kara and I sat outside together. Los Angeles was eerily quiet—no traffic, no yelling, no sense of movement anywhere. Everything felt strange and unfamiliar, and we didn't have answers. We just talked about whatever came to mind, trying to make sense of what was happening. At one point, she looked at me and asked, "What are you feeling?"

After sitting with the question for a few moments, the only words I could find were, "I feel like I'm disappearing."

The life I had worked so hard to rebuild was disappearing. The picture I carried of how this season would unfold—the book deal, the speaking career, the big doors opening—was disappearing. Even my hope that life could be different felt like it was slipping away. It was as if the scaffolding of who I thought I was began to collapse.

Kara let my words hang there, then asked a question that has followed me ever since: "Can you trust it?"

At first, I didn't know what she meant. Trust what? Trust the collapse? Trust the loss of everything I thought I was building? Trust the disappearance of the life I had imagined? But as the days turned into weeks, I began to ask what it would look like to trust the disappearance and stop fighting against it. Over time, I began to understand that trusting the disappearance meant trusting what came in its place—heaviness. Not the heaviness of being busy or burned out, but the ache that settles in when reality no longer matches the picture you've been holding. The deep sorrow that shows up when the life you thought you were living is gone, and the new one hasn't yet taken shape.

For most of my life, I had done everything I could to outrun that heaviness. I tried to heal it, outperform it, even pray it away. I believed that feeling the heaviness was an indication that something was wrong with me, with my faith, with my life. But in this season, I began to wonder if it was the opposite. I started to relate to heaviness the way the earth relates to gravity—not as a curse, but as something essential and true.

On July 30, 2020, I wrote the following in my journal:

What if things aren't supposed to change? What if this ache, this heaviness, that always finds its way back into my life, is actually the lover I've been looking for? What if she has something to say, and if I actually started to listen—if I actually engaged in the conversation instead of shutting down—I'd be able to put to words what my heart has been trying to say all along? And as a result, I wouldn't feel so misunderstood. What if me trying to rid myself of her, this heaviness, through more work and more healing, is actually doing me a disservice, leaving me feeling more broken and alone than before? What if I learned how to welcome and receive her with open arms, an open heart? What

> *if I allowed myself to get close enough to her so that I could kiss her with the same passion I would kiss a lover? Get naked with her and curl up to her and feel the warmth of her pressed up against my body. What if I fully accepted her, surrendering to her strong embrace, and allowed her to have her way with me? What if it's through this sacred union, this radical acceptance, that I begin to realize there's nothing wrong with me?*

With tears streaming down my face, I felt something open up inside me. The old striving—the endless need to be further along, to prove I was okay, to show that all my healing had been worth it—finally began to loosen its grip. The shift wasn't about figuring something out. It was about finally stopping the fight. I stopped trying to get rid of the heaviness and, for the first time, gave myself permission to be honest about what I was carrying.

It was in that honesty that I was finally able to confront the grief I had been carrying and begin to release the story of the life I thought I would have by now. When I spoke to Kara about it later, I realized that moment hadn't come because I had figured something out. It came because I stopped resisting the weight of what I was carrying. I stopped fighting against it, and I gave myself permission to be honest. The story didn't unfold the way I had planned or hoped. My expectations had never become a reality. I welcomed the heaviness not as a failure, but as a guest and as a guide.

And while it didn't disappear or evaporate into peace and clarity, it softened. The heaviness stopped pushing against me the moment I stopped pushing against it. In that moment of softening, something awakened within me. I experienced a sense of relief, as though I had been holding my breath for years and finally let it out. In that exhale, an inner peace emerged that had long been absent from my life.

We live in a culture that tells us heaviness is a problem to solve, not a truth to listen to. If it lingers too long, we assume something is wrong. We grow impatient with it, so we medicate it, numb it, outwork it, or hide it behind a smile. Because of that, we rarely learn how to sit with grief, disappointment, or loss. But heaviness isn't just an obstacle—it's a signpost. It shows up when something meaningful is being touched—when there's a loss to grieve, truth to face, or a life to let go of.

The danger of our impatience with heaviness is that it keeps us shallow. When we rush to get rid of what's heavy, we never stay with it long enough to learn from it. It disconnects us from the depth that offers us a more abundant life experience. As a result, we glide along the surface of our lives, all the while yearning for something deeper and more fulfilling. We end up mistaking busyness for meaning, noise for connection, and progress for growth. Yet beneath all the distractions lies a persistent ache—an ache that serves as an invitation to delve into the depths we have been evading.

You can see this pattern everywhere. You can see it in the way we rush to optimize instead of asking harder questions and the way we treat discomfort as a weakness instead of as a signal. We choose the quick fix over the honest reckoning, again and again. We're escape artists. Always moving faster, buying more, and chasing the next achievement while the very ache that could guide us toward emotional depth gets buried alive.

The irony is that the very heaviness we try to avoid can bring us back into contact with what is most human, most alive, most true. When we welcome heaviness instead of running from it, we not only find our own healing, but we begin to undo a cultural script that has left so many of us starved for depth.

Soulcraft

Up until this point in my journey, I had been slowly learning how to trust the disappearance. In Canada, I had learned to be still. In Los Angeles, I learned to let go of the picture I had imagined my life was supposed to look like. In both seasons, I began to understand that heaviness was not an enemy but a guide. But it wasn't until I encountered the work of Bill Plotkin and his book *Soulcraft* that I began to see the larger arc of my unstriving process.

I stumbled across the book not long after the world shut down in 2020. I don't even remember how it found me. Maybe it was an algorithm, maybe it was grace. Regardless, once I opened it, I couldn't put it down. Plotkin was writing about something I had already been living but didn't yet have language for. He called it the path of descent. In a culture obsessed with ascent, this almost felt subversive. We live in a world that celebrates what's rising—growth, expansion, visibility, progress. Even our spiritual language mirrors this: awakening, elevation, transcendence, becoming higher versions of ourselves. The assumption is that a good life moves up and to the right. But soul doesn't live there.

Instead of climbing higher, Plotkin's approach to life was about falling deeper. Instead of chasing achievement, it was about surrendering to initiation. And as I read, I realized that this was the through line of my own experience. From football to Canada to Los Angeles, I was on the path of descent.

But descent is not the end goal. Descent is only the pathway. We descend not for the sake of suffering, but because only in the depths can soul reveal itself. When life strips away our plans, identities, and false securities, it creates the emptiness where something wilder and more authentic can be born. That is why heaviness, loss, and collapse matter—they press us downward, away from performance and pretense, toward the deeper currents of who we are. They carve out the inner space where soul can find us.

And this is not just a poetic idea. It matters because without soul, we remain trapped in cycles of striving and survival. We keep performing, producing, and proving, all while quietly wondering why it still doesn't feel like enough. Soul can interrupt that cycle. It roots us in something larger than ambition. It gives us direction and meaning that achievement alone can never deliver. It shifts the question from "How do I get ahead?" to "What am I here to give?"

That realization changed everything for me. Even after leaving striving behind, I still carried the pressure to constantly figure out what was next, to find the calling that would make sense of all I had lost. But what Plotkin helped me see is that soul does not respond to effort. It doesn't arrive through force. It emerges when we stop climbing and allow ourselves to be carried downward. It is born in disappearance.

Plotkin described soul not as a career or a brand to build, but as an ecological niche, a mythic role we are born to play in the larger earth community. He wrote that soul is not something we choose. It is something that claims us when we are willing to be still and vulnerable enough to be found.

My intense connection with this material is what eventually led me to sign up for a weeklong Soulcraft intensive, as a gift for my fortieth birthday. I didn't go to get answers—I went to make myself available to be found. More than anything, I wanted to put myself in a context where soul could claim me.

On the third night of the intensive, I found myself unable to sleep, feeling frustrated as the anticipated encounter with my soul remained elusive. As I lay in my tent late at night, there was a stirring in me to go and wander. I tried to dismiss it, but I couldn't. Although I couldn't articulate what I was feeling, I recognized the need to move my body. So I unzipped my tent, and I began to wander into the dark.

After some time, I emerged into a wide clearing on top of a hillside. The sky stretched above me, and the trees formed a silent circle all around. I had wandered the land the previous two days, but I had never stood in this exact place. Something about it felt holy. I stood there for a moment, fully aware that while I couldn't see into the forest, I was completely exposed to it. I could feel the eyes of the more-than-human world watching. I felt deeply vulnerable, and in that vulnerability, I felt a question emerge from deep within me.

Would I allow myself to be fully seen and trust the darkness?

I didn't know exactly what that meant, but I knew what I needed to do. I wanted to signal to the universe that I was all in. So I removed my clothes as a gesture of trust. Yes, you read that right—I was butt naked in the middle of the wilderness at two in the morning. If a park ranger had stumbled across me, I'd still be trying to explain myself. Then I took out a small rattle I had brought with me, and I began to shake it while standing fully nude in the clearing. It was my way of saying, "I'm here. I'm willing. I'm listening."

The vulnerability that washed over me in that moment was unlike anything I had ever experienced. Physically, emotionally, spiritually—I was exposed. Every part of me wanted to run back to the safety of my tent, but I stayed. Deep down, I sensed that this was a turning point. My sole responsibility was not to instigate any action, but to stay present while embracing the emerging discomfort.

I was beginning to see that life's seasons weren't rushing me into what was next but were growing my inner capacity to stay with the unknown long enough for something real to take shape. Disappearance isn't about speed. It's about patience, trust, and learning to stand in the dark until the new life announces itself.

Later in the week, I remembered a word from the Inuit tradition: *qarrtsiluni.* The Inuit are Indigenous peoples of the Arctic regions of Canada, Greenland, and Alaska, whose lives for centuries have been bound to the rhythms of the land, sea, and ice. *Qarrtsiluni* means "sitting together in the darkness, waiting for something to burst forth."

For generations, hunters would gather in silence, with no fire or light, waiting for the call of the whale. Their lives and the lives of those in their community depended on the whale as the very source of life, feeding the entire community. But they never knew when, or if, the call would come. So they waited, not with passivity, but with a reverence and a readiness that sharpened their attention.

Qarrtsiluni is not about trying harder, nor is it about giving up. It's about surrendering to the dark long enough for life to speak in its own timing. You cannot predict it. You cannot control it. You cannot force it into being. You can only show up open and vulnerable, waiting for the universe to deliver what you cannot make happen on your own.

And that is the same posture disappearance asks of us. When the life you thought you were living collapses, when the picture in your head dissolves, when all you can feel is heaviness—you cannot force your way through it. You can only wait. Not out of resignation, but in reverence. Wait and trust something will rise, even if you do not know when or what it will be.

Looking back to my wilderness retreat experience, that's what I was doing that night. I sat naked on the ground, waiting for something that might never come. It made no sense, but it felt sacred. For nearly an hour, I called out without knowing who or what I was calling to, only that I was making myself available. And then it happened. A coyote's howl split the silence. It sounded so close, I undoubtedly knew it was for me. With tears in my eyes, I put on my clothes, packed up my bag, and started walking back to my tent.

It's easy to talk about trusting the disappearance and the darkness that comes with it in theory. It's something else entirely to choose to sit in it, exposed, and stay in it for as long as it takes to hear something new. And that's what this season of my life was teaching me. To stop striving for the next answer and instead, make an altar out of the unknowing. To stop chasing the path and let the path find me.

To wait in the clearing long enough for the howl to rise.

The Well of Grief

When I first entered this season, I thought life was merciless. I thought I was being punished for mistakes I couldn't undo. The collapse of my plans and the disappearance of what I thought was coming next felt like proof that I had been left behind. But now, I see it differently. What felt merciless was actually kindness.

The deeper into my own journey I go, the more I see that the heartbeat of life is expansion. Life loves us too much to let us stay small, so it keeps leading us out of the houses we've built, beyond the pictures we've been carrying, into a territory we don't yet recognize. It is a circular rhythm. We build; we let go. We belong; we leave. We become; we are undone. Each time we think we've arrived, life opens the door again and asks us to step further inside.

At first, the darkness will convince us something is wrong—with us, with the path, with the world. And everything in us will want to run back inside and reconstruct what is familiar. But if we can stay long enough in the vulnerability of that darkness, something will begin to shift. We'll realize the darkness is holy. It isn't empty at all—it's spacious. It's full of mercy and grace as it creates the room that the next version of our life requires.

I was talking with a friend recently about her own season of disappearance, and she asked me, "Do we really have to go through this over and over again?" I answered, as gently as I could, yes. Disappearance is always the prerequisite for what's next. The emptying always comes before the becoming. And while these seasons may not get easier, we learn to resist them less. And when we resist less, we begin to participate more. We stop clinging to what's falling away and start honoring the sacred rhythm of what's being born.

A few months before Kara and I left Los Angeles, I sat on a bench overlooking the Pacific Ocean, thinking about how I once imagined my healing would lead me into a bigger life. I thought the doors would open, the opportunities would line up, and the future I imagined would finally arrive. But as I sat there, I realized this part of my journey was never about building a bigger life. It was about learning how to inhabit the one I already had.

For years in LA, I was always peeking around the corner, waiting for my life to finally begin. But through disappearance and grief, I began to see that life had been there the entire time—I just hadn't been living it.

We tend to honor the visionaries, the dreamers, the ones reaching for what's next—and they matter. That way of seeing the world carries its own wisdom. But there's also wisdom in learning how to live the life that's already here. To stay present to the ordinary moments without needing them to become something else in order to feel meaningful.

That's no small thing in a culture that constantly pulls our attention toward what's new, improved, and just out of reach. We're surrounded by images of the life we could be living, the versions of ourselves we're supposed to become, the next thing that promises to finally make us feel more alive. It trains us to live one step ahead of our own lives.

This is the gift of the disappearance. It interrupts that forward pull and collapses the illusion that fulfillment lives somewhere else. It strips away what's false—not to punish us, but to return us to what's true. And in that stripping away, we begin to see that this life—imperfect, unfinished, ordinary as it is—has always been, is, and will always be, more than enough.

Maybe you're there now. Maybe you've pulled the cord, everything familiar has fallen away, and you are in free fall, unsure if anything will catch you. If that's where you are, feeling lost in the season of disappearance, and nothing new has shown up, trust the heaviness and follow your grief.

It will lead you home.

A Gentle Invitation

If you find yourself in a season of disappearance, start by humanizing your grief. For me, my grief's name is Grace. Now imagine Grace sitting across from you at a table. If you were willing to meet her, whether she is the grief of a relationship that didn't last, or a dream that never took shape, or a life you thought you'd be living by now, what would you want to say to her? And just as important—what might she want to say to you? If you want a good place to start, here are two journal prompts I use often:

Grace, what hurts the most is . . .

Grace, what I didn't expect to grieve was . . .

This simple act of naming and welcoming your grief can become a doorway. Open it and see that, even here, life has not abandoned you. Something is already at work beneath the surface, shaping you for what's next. Trust the disappearance.

Chapter Eight

NOTHING LEFT TO HIDE

We may become strangers to those who thought they knew us, but at least we are no longer strangers to ourselves.

—James Hollis

We were only a few weeks into dating when Kara and I were lying in bed in her tiny garage-turned-apartment in West Hollywood, asking each other playful questions. We had been moving through childhood memories and favorite ice cream flavors when the conversation turned toward sex. In an instant, everything inside of me changed. The lightness disappeared, a tightness spread across my chest, and I could feel myself starting to shut down.

For years, sex had been my escape. When life felt unmanageable, when I felt weak or overwhelmed, I reached for a new partner. It gave me a rush of control, as if I could flip the balance of power and prove I wasn't as powerless as I felt. In the moment, it would feel like I was steering my own life again, but afterward, I would stand in the shower, scrubbing my skin as if I could wash away the shame that clung to me.

And now, here I was, lying next to the woman I wanted to build a life with, gripped by the fear that if she really knew my past, she would no longer want me. Her sexual history was minimal, while mine, in a very big way, felt like a long list of regrets. In that moment, I was convinced I was too dirty, too broken, too unworthy of the kind of love I so desperately wanted and felt with Kara.

I started to panic while trying to change the subject. I could feel the weight of it pressing against me, rising higher the more I tried to push it down. Everything in me wanted to disappear. In the past, I would have turned to anger as my escape hatch, shutting down any situation where I felt exposed or vulnerable. But this time, the anger wasn't there. All I could feel was the overwhelming urge to shut down and hide.

Kara noticed immediately. She saw the shift in my body, the way I tried to get small, the way I was pulling away, and how my eyes avoided hers. Instead of recoiling, she leaned closer. She searched my face for a moment, taking me in with a softness and compassion, and then softly asked, "Are you feeling shame?"

Before I could speak, the tears came. I prepared myself for rejection, but it never came. She didn't try to fix me or interrogate me or smooth things over. She just stayed with me in the vulnerability of the moment. Then she did something I will never forget. She leaned in even closer and began blowing gently across my face.

It startled me at first, and when I asked what she was doing, she smiled and said, "I'm blowing away the shame. It doesn't belong here."

In that instant, something shifted. I had just experienced a depth of connection not as a reward for keeping it together or proving myself worthy, but as a gift given to me exactly as I was. Kara wasn't responding to the polished version of me; she was loving the raw and unguarded one.

For most of my life, I thought strength was about pushing through the doubt, fear, and exhaustion while outrunning the parts of myself I didn't want anyone to see. But that experience showed me something different. What drew me into real connection wasn't pushing harder—it was allowing. Allowing myself to be seen. Allowing myself to be loved. Allowing myself to remain in the mess of the moment and discover that I wasn't disqualified from true, deep, accepting love after all.

No Image Left to Manage

That night with Kara wasn't just about intimacy. It revealed the pattern that had been running my entire life—the instinct to shrink, protect myself, and control the story when I felt vulnerable and exposed.

For years, I had lived as if my survival depended on tightly managing the image of who I was. If I looked strong enough, disciplined enough, or successful enough, then maybe I'd deserve to be loved. If I hid the messy parts, then maybe I'd stay safe. But managing a great image isn't the same as living a great life, and survival by image management comes at a great cost. Because when you sink everything into forcing belonging—silencing what feels like too much, and polishing what feels like not enough—there's no energy left for the real experience of being alive.

We live in a culture that rewards this behavior. Social media makes it easy to curate yourself into someone admirable. Most companies don't want their employees' authenticity—they simply want their productivity to keep the machine moving. Families learn to show the highlight reel while burying the dysfunction. Everything around us whispers the same message—keep the mask on, because being fully human is too much.

This is why it feels like death when the mask finally falls away. At first, it feels like failure. You're standing fully naked in the rawness of life, without the familiar armor of achievement, competence, or control. The part of you that learned to survive by performing panics, because it doesn't know who you are without the protection. But buried in that discomfort is the relief of having nothing left to manage. Because when it all falls away, all that's left is you.

We think freedom comes from accumulation—from stacking more achievements, polishing our skills, gathering more proof of our success. But the freedom we long for doesn't come from accumulation. It comes from a shedding, when the layers we've built to survive finally fall away, and we're left standing in what's real.

I didn't have language for it at the time, but one of the first places I saw this in action was in *8 Mile,* a movie I watched on repeat in my early twenties. At the end, in the final rap battle, Eminem doesn't win by hiding his flaws. He takes the microphone and names them all—his failures, his shame, and the humiliations his opponent was going to throw at him. By owning them out loud, he disarms the attack. There's nothing left to weaponize.

That's the gift of nothing left to hide. When the image collapses, when there's no polish left to protect you, you realize the very thing you thought would ruin you is what finally frees you. You stop living to manage perception, and you start learning what it means to belong to yourself.

But, in order to get to that place, we have to cross the threshold of loneliness.

The Threshold of Loneliness

The moment we stop managing our image is the moment the ground beneath us shifts. At first, it feels like freedom. A weight lifts, and the mask loosens. We take a deep breath we didn't know we were holding. But not long after, something else often comes rushing in—loneliness.

This loneliness is not just about being without company. It is the ache and discomfort of standing in the unfamiliar space between identities. The self you used to be is slowly disappearing, and the new self hasn't taken shape yet. You're suspended in between, belonging nowhere, not even fully to yourself.

This loneliness feels existential and can cut deeply. It's not just "I am alone tonight." It's "I don't know who I am now, or how to find my way in this room, in this life." And because you no longer recognize yourself, you can't be sure others will recognize you either. The people who once *knew* you may not know how to relate to the you you're becoming. Because of this, relationships stumble and conversations feel off-balance, like you're speaking a language no one else understands. You walk through your life feeling misunderstood and deeply unknown.

It doesn't help that everything around us insists loneliness should be treated like a problem to solve. We scroll and swipe, buy and binge, filling the emptiness with noise and calling it connection. We tell people to join more groups, get busier, be more social—as if the cure for loneliness is simply more company. We pathologize it, as though it were a sickness, when in truth it is part of being human. We shame and judge it, suggesting that if you feel lonely, you must not be lovable. Loneliness has no place to simply be held.

But ignoring the loneliness doesn't make it disappear. It can leak out as rage, as scapegoating, or as the constant demand for an enemy to blame. A culture that refuses to face its loneliness will keep turning its grief into violence and its ache into division. This is why learning to stay with your own loneliness is not just personal work—it is cultural repair.

Just as a culture cannot heal what it refuses to face, neither can we. The pull is always to run back, to patch up the old mask, and return to the familiar patterns of approval at whatever cost. But what I've realized in my years of traversing the landscape of loneliness is that it's necessary. It's the ground between false belonging and true belonging, between survival and something more alive. If you stay put and are willing to befriend the loneliness, it begins to transform.

When I refer to this as sacred ground, it's not because it feels good. It's because it's holy work. Loneliness strips away the roles we use to secure approval, as there's no one to impress. It's the desert where distractions dry up, and our false belonging dies, leaving only the truth. It is the cave where we stop reaching for someone else to complete us and begin to learn how to be with ourselves without escape.

Sacred does not mean easy. Sacred means necessary. If you can stay with loneliness—if you can bear the weight of its silence long enough—it begins to soften into belonging. First to yourself, then, slowly, to others who can meet you there.

The Belonging We Crave

In the story "A Painful Case," by Irish writer James Joyce, there's a man named Mr. Duffy who is a rigid, overly rational man who lives a small, quiet life, keeping people and emotions at a safe distance. At one point, he has the chance for real intimacy, but he turns it down. The risk of being seen felt more dangerous than the certainty of staying hidden. Years later, when that window of connection had closed, he withdrew into himself, cut off from his own life. Joyce described him with one unforgettable line: *"Mr. Duffy lived a short distance from his body."*

I connect with Joyce's writing because he has a talent for cutting straight to the heart of what it means to be human. That line names more than a single character's fate—it names us. We live in a culture that trains us to stay just far enough away from ourselves to function but never close enough to feel fully alive. We manage and numb. We curate and polish. We keep enough distance to avoid being exposed. It works well enough to get by, but the deeper cost is that you can maintain life from a distance, but you can never belong there unless you participate.

This is the deeper sickness of our age. Belonging has been

hollowed out and sold back to us as branding, political identity, and curated community. We are told that to belong we must wear the right mask, say the right lines, and hold the right opinions. We are rewarded for conformity and punished for depth. Because these versions of belonging are thin, we cling to them even tighter. We build belonging around slogans and symbols. We divide the world into insiders and outsiders. The very hunger for connection that could draw us closer together becomes the fuel for an *us-versus-them* existence. What we're left with is not true community but rival camps, each defending its own fragile sense of worth. The result is an epidemic of loneliness disguised as connection.

False belonging produces fragile people. When your identity depends on a slogan or a crowd, you cannot bear complexity. You cannot carry your own fear, grief, or pain, so you project it outward. Fragile people create fragile systems—politics, workplaces, even families that fracture under pressure. True belonging, by contrast, produces durable people. People who can hold differences without panic, face loss without scapegoating, and stand in the complexity of being human without reducing themselves or others. This is not just about you—it's about the kind of world we create together.

But what makes true belonging so elusive is that it is not something a culture can manufacture for you, nor something a crowd can grant. It is not the reward for being agreeable enough, likable enough, or polished enough. What is offered as belonging today are only substitutes—short-lived affirmations that collapse as soon as we step out of line. Yet we settle for those substitutes because they feel safer than the vulnerability it would take to seek out the real thing. It is easier to shrink yourself into a slogan than to risk being known in your depth. A slogan is simple, clean, and easy to defend. But a life reduced to slogans cannot hold the sorrow, the grief, the fear, and the pain that make you human. When you cut those parts off, you don't escape them—you only exile yourself from the kind of belonging that truly nourishes your soul.

True belonging takes courage. This is why most people will go their entire lives without ever tasting it. It will always be easier to retreat and wear the mask. It takes less risk to repeat the slogans, to hold the right opinions, or to let a group decide who you are. That kind of belonging costs little, but it also gives little.

Real belonging asks you to step out from behind the mask and face the insecurities it was hiding. It asks you to stop reducing yourself to slogans and instead learn how to carry the whole of who you are. It asks you to allow your grief and fear to sit alongside your joy and strength, without erasing or explaining them away. It asks you to risk being known in that wholeness, even when it feels easier to fake it and leave the rest in the shadows.

This is what our culture has forgotten or, worse yet, never experienced. Belonging is not built on sameness or performance, but on your willingness to bring the parts of yourself you once buried into the light. It asks for nothing less than your whole self and the decision to live with nothing left to hide. Until you risk giving yourself up fully, you will live like Mr. Duffy—close enough to appear alive, but just far enough away to miss the marrow of your own life.

Living from Belonging

Belonging to yourself doesn't just heal the past; it reshapes how you move into the future. Once you discover that you can live with nothing left to hide and still be loved, a new kind of strength begins to grow in you. It isn't the bravado of pretending you're untouchable, and it isn't the false confidence of never doubting again. It's subtler than that, but also steadier. It is the realization that no matter what happens, you will not abandon yourself.

That realization is the foundation of self-trust. Self-trust is simply the confidence that when life tests you, you will stay true to yourself instead of betraying yourself. It's knowing you can hold your own fear without numbing it, that you can speak the truth you once swallowed, and that you can stand in the discomfort of vulnerability without scrambling for your familiar mask.

Day-to-day, self-trust looks like choosing rest when the old voice in the back of your head is still trying to convince you that your worth depends on working harder. It looks like setting a boundary in a relationship instead of silencing your needs to keep the peace. It looks like telling the truth in a meeting, even when your voice shakes. It looks like staying present in your grief instead of outrunning it with busyness. It looks like catching yourself in a moment you'd normally abandon ship—and choosing, this time, to be present with what is.

This kind of trust changes everything because you will never be able to predict how life will unfold. There will always be uncertainty. There will be losses, detours, and seasons that refuse to cooperate. You can get through those seasons by relying on your masks, group membership, and false belonging. Most people do. But that kind of belonging comes with a tradeoff. The more you rely on external belonging to feel safe, the less access you have to the deeper rewards of being alive—connection, freedom, and self-respect. You survive, but you don't get the gold.

When you know that you can trust yourself, things shift. You stop organizing your life around certainty and start organizing it around integrity. You no longer need certainty to move forward because you know that whatever you face, you trust yourself.

This is bigger than personal resilience—it is cultural resistance. We live in a world that teaches us to outsource our trust—trust the market, trust the brand, trust the crowd, trust the image. When those collapse, we collapse with them. But self-trust cannot be taken away, because it is built on the unshakable decision to remain faithful to your own life.

A culture of self-abandonment produces fragile people—easily swayed by noise, quick to divide into insiders and outsiders, desperate for approval. But a person who has learned to belong to themselves carries a different presence. They can enter conflict without needing to win, hold grief without rushing to fix it, and meet differences without turning them into the enemy. They become trustworthy to others because they are no longer betraying themselves.

This is why belonging matters. It is not self-indulgence. It is the foundation of integrity, courage, and real community. Until you learn to belong to yourself, you'll never truly know who you really are. You will stay loyal to the false self, clinging to the approval of others, and call it a life—while the potential for a more expansive life waiting within you withers.

But when you refuse to abandon yourself and discover a true sense of belonging, you begin to live from a steadiness that no failure can undo. You walk into uncertainty without guarantees, and you can be misunderstood without coming undone. This is the freedom of belonging to yourself. Because while the false self might keep you alive, it will never allow you to truly live.

A Gentle Invitation

If you want to start living with nothing left to hide, don't try to tell the whole truth of your life all at once.

That usually backfires. Start with one small place where you already know you're not being fully honest.

It might be:

- A relationship where you keep things light when they're not.
- A habit of saying "It's fine" when it isn't.
- A place where you agree quickly so you don't have to deal with tension later.

For the next week, practice saying what you mean instead of what comes out automatically. That might sound like:

- "I don't know yet."
- "I need more time to think about that."
- "I said yes too fast."
- "I'm not great today."

Each time you tell the truth instead of abandoning yourself, you give yourself evidence that you can tell the truth and the ground doesn't fall out from under you. Over time, those moments of evidence add up. This is how we start living with nothing left to hide.

Chapter Nine

THE ILLUSION OF SAFETY

In the middle of winter, I at last discovered that there was in me an invincible summer.

— Albert Camus

Not too long ago, I hit a big milestone in my speaking business. In one single day, I booked four engagements totaling nearly $50,000—contracts signed and deposits sent. At the time, that was almost more than I had made in my first two full years of speaking. I leaned back in my chair, staring at the screen, and let myself feel it. A smile stretched across my face because, for the first time in a long time, I wasn't just surviving this work, I was expanding it. This was the kind of day that made the long stretches of doubt and persistence feel worth it.

I looked at the clock and saw it was close to five. Kara was out with the kids, the house was quiet, and I thought to myself, *This moment deserves a celebratory cocktail.* I walked over to the bar cart, grabbed the cocktail shaker, and started to pull bottles from the top shelf. But a few moments later, something in me hesitated. It was so small I almost ignored it, but the hesitation lingered, and all I could ask myself was, *Why am I celebrating myself by poisoning myself?*

This question wasn't about alcohol. I wasn't making a vow to quit or wrestling with the idea of sobriety. It was something deeper, even though I couldn't necessarily name what it was right away. I put the shaker back down and sat down on the couch. The pride I had felt only moments earlier was still there, but it was now mixed with a strange unease.

When I closed my eyes and listened, I could feel something beneath the joy, a kind of tension I hadn't noticed until this moment. It was faint, like a silent alarm in the background. I couldn't name it in that moment, but the success I had just experienced didn't settle in the way I thought it would. If I were being honest with myself, it made me restless, exposed, and a little on edge. I sat with it for a while, confused by what I was feeling, until it dawned on me that I wasn't reaching for a drink to celebrate. I was reaching for a drink to soften the sharpness of the joy I was feeling in the moment.

This realization gripped and confused me. Why would I want to mute something I had worked so hard to create? Why would I shrink from the very moment I had been waiting for? I didn't have words for it then, but I know now that what was happening inside me wasn't about the alcohol—it was my nervous system sounding the alarm. More success meant more visibility. More visibility meant more risk of being criticized, more pressure to deliver, more chances to fall short. Even though in my head I loved the idea of greater success, my nervous system equated this visibility with danger, and it was treating this breakthrough not as a gift but as a threat.

So there I was, sitting on the couch in my living room, staring at the cocktail shaker on the counter, when I realized something I had never put together before. Inner safety isn't only what we need to get through storms. Inner safety is what makes it possible to hold the fullness of a breakthrough moment, the joy, the visibility, the pressure, the risk, without shutting down. Without it, even the richness of the life that we've longed for can feel overwhelming, and we might find ourselves numbing or shrinking to take the edge off. We might call it celebrating when, in fact, it's us trying to bring our lives back down to a size our nervous system knows how to manage.

The Capacity Ceiling

I grew up believing that if I could build enough—more success, more achievement, more stability—then I'd finally feel safe. But the truth is often the opposite. The higher we climb, the more fragile life can feel, because we have more to lose. What we think will steady us can actually make us anxious and restless, endlessly bracing for a fall that may or may not come.

This is where the capacity ceiling comes in. The capacity ceiling is the invisible line inside us that decides how much stress we can bear before shutting down and how much joy, success, love, or goodness we can hold before it feels unsafe. We keep reaching for more, believing it will finally bring us safety, yet when it arrives, our nervous system often treats it like a threat. The very thing we said we wanted suddenly feels too vulnerable, too exposed, or too risky. Without even realizing it, we begin to shrink the moment down to a size that feels safer.

You've probably experienced this before. The relationship seemed too good to be true, so you found yourself picking fights or pulling away. The opportunity you worked so hard for, only to second-guess yourself the moment it arrived. The urge to sabotage, distract, or numb whenever things finally start to go your way. These aren't failures of discipline or character. They are signs that you have bumped up against your capacity ceiling.

The capacity ceiling doesn't appear out of nowhere. It forms early, shaped by our nervous system's early survival education. For some of us, joy was met with "Calm down" or "Don't get carried away." For others, like me, success drew criticism, envy, or pressure to keep performing. Even affection sometimes came with strings attached. Little by little, our bodies learned that too much good brings risk. What started as protection hardened into a habit. The nervous system set an internal threshold that said *This much is safe; more than this is dangerous.*

What's important to understand is that capacity ceilings don't lift through willpower. They don't move because we try harder, and you can't force growth through more effort. Ceilings move when the nervous system learns that more is safe. Without safety, effort just reinforces the ceiling. With safety, the ceiling dissolves on its own.

I see this play out with my daughter, Sophie. She's three and a half, and lately she's been climbing up on the couch or playground equipment, working up the courage to jump. At first, the jumps were tiny. She needed me right there, arms open, promising to catch her. But the more she experienced the ground holding her, and the more she felt the safety of my arms when she landed, the braver she became. Her jumps grew bigger. She stretched into what once felt impossible, not because the ground had changed, but because she knew she was safe enough to risk it.

That's exactly how our nervous system works with success. At first, the leap into something bigger feels terrifying. We don't yet trust that we'll be caught. But each time we stay present through the fear instead of pulling back, we teach the little boy or girl inside us that it's safe to hold more. Safe to be seen. Safe to succeed. Safe to love. And slowly, our jumps get bigger. We move from stress to stretch, and that stretch lifts our capacity ceiling. It teaches our nervous system that we can step into greater success without collapsing, just as Sophie's body learned she could leap higher because she trusted my arms to hold her.

This is why so many of us can build lives that look full and successful yet still feel weighed down inside. We build outward, stacking more onto our lives without strengthening the foundation beneath it all. Eventually, the life we've constructed feels fragile, or even too heavy to carry. Not because we lack the ability to do more, but because our capacity ceiling has never been stretched.

This is the illusion of safety. We chase success believing it will finally allow us to exhale. More money, more recognition, more control—then we'll feel settled. But success increases demand. The responsibilities grow, the exposure widens, and the stakes rise. If our internal capacity doesn't grow alongside our external success, the nervous system doesn't relax—it stays hyper-vigilant. What we hoped would make us feel safer starts to feel heavier. We can't enjoy what we've built because we're too busy enduring it.

For me, that endurance showed up most clearly in how I related to joy. For a long time, I didn't realize how little joy I allowed myself to feel. When things were going well, I stayed on high alert, always ready for the next shoe to drop. I couldn't fully relax into good moments because my tolerance for joy was so small. Celebration felt risky, and ease felt temporary. Even happiness carried a low-grade vigilance. It wasn't humility—it was a nervous system that had learned to associate joy with danger. Living that way, always preparing for loss instead of embodying the joy available, was a miserable way to live.

The good news is the ceiling isn't fixed in place. It isn't a glass wall we are doomed to keep bumping against. It's more like a muscle that can be stretched with care. Every time we notice the urge to numb or shrink, every time we pause long enough to breathe through the discomfort and stay open, we are teaching our nervous system that it is safe to hold more. More joy. More success. More love. More of life itself.

This is the real work of safety. It isn't about removing risk or controlling outcomes. It's about realizing that as life expands, the nervous system has to expand with it. Because life will always ask more of us—more courage, more presence, and more trust. If we don't stretch our ceiling, we might achieve what we once wanted, but we will never be able to settle into it. Most importantly, we'll never be able to fully enjoy it.

I invite you to stop trying to outrun vulnerability and to instead build the inner foundation that allows you to face it. When we do, the ceiling lifts and with it, our ability to live more freely.

Rune

The same illusion that drives us to chase more success to feel secure is the illusion that shatters the moment life refuses to follow our plans. I learned this the night Kara's phone rang, and everything we thought we knew about our second child's future was shaken.

We were expecting the same kind of call we had received with Sophie—a nurse on the line, cheerful and excited, ready to reveal the gender. That night, as we sat at the kitchen island, Kara's phone lit up. She smiled and told me to set up my phone to record the moment.

Instead of a nurse's voice, it was our doctor. Her tone was calm but heavy, and I knew this wasn't just a happy update. There was something else going on. Almost immediately, without warning, our doctor told us that we were having a son. Then she paused and said, "But I also need to tell you about the other results we found in your blood test." The test showed a genetic condition, one she couldn't fully explain. The spectrum was wide. Some boys live without ever knowing they have it. Others require constant care. "We just don't know yet," she said.

Until that moment, I had believed I had finally built a life that felt steady. I was speaking, writing, and creating work I loved. Our home life felt good. For the first time in years, I wasn't waiting for the floor to collapse beneath me. I told myself, *This is it. This is safe.* For years, I thought security came from stacking more on top of itself—a bigger career, a better life, more stability. But that night showed me the truth. What I had built was a glass house, and one phone call was enough to reveal how fragile it really was. What collapsed wasn't my life, but the belief that external stability could protect me from uncertainty.

When the call ended, I wrapped Kara in my arms and told her we would be okay. But inside, I split in two. Part of me was there, holding her. The other part raced ahead, preparing for the worst. My oldest reflex when fear shows up has always been control—make plans, stay strong, try to get ahead of vulnerability.

In the weeks that followed, I buried myself in work. I filled every gap with noise. At home, I was short, distracted, and picking fights about open cabinet doors and laundry. None of it was about cabinets or laundry. It was about the fear I couldn't name. Kara and I were surviving side by side, but we weren't living our lives together.

Eventually, I couldn't outrun it anymore. One afternoon, I asked Kara if we could sit down so I could tell her the truth, and I did. I told her I was afraid. I told her I was angry—angry that life could be so fragile, angry that I had ever believed I could build a life safe from disruption. Saying it out loud felt vulnerable but also empowering. Because of that honesty, something shifted between us. The heaviness eased, and in its place, we discovered trust—trust that even without answers, we could face the unknown together. Not trust that things would turn out a certain way, but trust that we could remain connected no matter how they did. That trust felt sturdier than anything I had tried to build with control. It gave us ground we could actually stand on, not because our situation had changed, but because we had changed.

We still live with uncertainty about our son Rune's future. But because we continue to build that inner safety—within ourselves and within our relationship—we've been able to trade the fear of what might happen for the joy that is already here. We're able to live—not just brace for survival—while holding immense gratitude for everything along the way.

Not long after learning the news about my son, I was reading *The Little Tree* to Sophie before bed. Page after page, I felt something softening in me. The story is about a young tree that grows its first leaves in spring, then faces its first winter. All the other trees let go, trusting something new will come. The little tree clings. It doesn't want to lose what it has, and because it won't release its leaves, it doesn't grow.

As I read those words aloud, I could feel the boy in me exhale. That was what this season was asking of me—to stop gripping so tightly to the version of safety I once believed would protect us, to let go of the leaves I had clung to, and to trust the winter I was in. Even winter brings its own kind of safety—it makes way for spring.

Creating Inner Safety

That season with Rune revealed how fragile my outer safety really was. It also invited me into the deeper work of building a safety that could not be taken from me. That work began, quite literally, in my own body. Real safety isn't found in achievements or guarantees. It's built in the moment-to-moment practice of staying with ourselves when life feels uncertain or overwhelming—through both the hard and the good.

Our autonomic nervous system (ANS) is the part of us that runs in the background, making decisions long before our mind catches up. It is the system that keeps our heart beating, our lungs expanding, and our digestion moving without our awareness. It is also the system that constantly scans the world around us, asking a single question: Am I safe?

This process happens so quickly and so far beneath our conscious thought that we rarely notice it, but it shapes our entire experience of life. When we move through our life, and the answer to *Am I safe?* is yes, our nervous system relaxes. We find ourselves present, connected, creative, and able to engage fully with the people and opportunities in front of us. When the answer is no, even if there is no real danger, the system shifts. We armor ourselves in the ways that once helped us survive, even if those same strategies now keep us from living.

I didn't understand this for most of my life. I thought my swings between weeks of relentless drive and days of collapse reflected a failure of discipline or willpower. In truth, they were the signs of a nervous system doing its best to protect me.

Researchers describe the ANS less like an on-off switch and more like a ladder. At the top is what's called the ventral state, where we feel steady and open enough to stay connected.

When the body senses threat, we move down into sympathetic activation—fight or flight. The heart pounds. The mind races. The body braces. Stay there long enough, and the system drops further into the lowest rung, called the dorsal state. This is the shutdown state—fatigue, numbness, withdrawal. From the outside, it may look like laziness or depression, but often it's the body's way of conserving what little energy it has left.

For many of us, this cycle has become the rhythm of modern life. We spend our days in sympathetic overdrive—rushing, producing, responding to demands—and then we go home, pour a drink, scroll a screen, or collapse on the couch and call it self-care. But what looks like rest is often just a shutdown. Our bodies aren't resting; they're retreating. Because we've normalized this pattern, we don't recognize it as dysregulation. We just call it ambition on one end and relaxation on the other, when in truth, it's the nervous system swinging between high alert and collapse.

For years, I cycled through these states without understanding what was happening. I believed hustle was strength, when in truth, my system was running from fear. I believed collapse was weakness, when in truth, I was collapsing from the exhaustion of being stuck in survival mode. What finally began to change my life was the lesson that these states are not permanent, and they are not failures. They are invitations to listen more closely to what my body is telling me.

This is why I say that real safety begins within. It is not about staying in the ventral state all the time. That is not realistic and not the goal. The goal is awareness. The goal is compassion. The goal is to know where we are on the ladder, to meet ourselves there with kindness instead of judgment, and to have the tools to adjust accordingly.

Part of the magic of the inner advantage loop you read about in chapter five is that it also seamlessly works as a framework for building inner safety. When disruption hits your life hard, or when your success feels too vulnerable to hold, these three moves give you a way to stay present with what you're feeling instead of collapsing or retreating.

Recognize when you've shifted out of balance. Notice the signals—your chest tightening, your breath shortening, feeling the urge to fix, perform, or disappear. Most of us blow past these cues until we've spiraled. Recognition is what interrupts the freefall.

Reframe the meaning of what's happening. Instead of shaming yourself for being weak or anxious, try to see the dysregulation as proof that you're brushing up against your current capacity ceiling. It's a sign your nervous system is doing its job, trying to keep you safe, and that you have an opportunity to expand what safety means.

Recenter by taking one small, grounding, tolerable step. Release a slow exhale. Name five things you see in the room. Put a hand on your heart and tell the younger part of you, *You are safe now.* These small shifts are how we teach the body that life is not something to brace against, and that both disruption and breakthrough can be held without collapse.

Now, the new goal is not to aim for a regulated life all the time. Life will always lift us up and pull us down the ladder in ways we can't anticipate. The work going forward is to notice when we've shifted, and to meet ourselves with awareness and care, instead of judgment. Each time we do, we lay another brick in the foundation of inner safety. Over time, what once felt overwhelming becomes manageable. What once seemed too good to trust becomes safe to receive. And that is the foundation of real emotional safety—not an illusion we attempt to build outside of us, but a strength that lives within and grows stronger the more we practice.

Inner safety not only stabilizes us during challenging times but also opens us up to receive more goodness than we previously believed life could hold. With more practice, I started to feel a new sense of space emerging within me. I could meet a more expansive life without trying to control it or rushing to shrink it down to something familiar. Before long, I was presented with an opportunity that revealed what is possible when you are able to embrace more.

The $100,000 Story

One evening, not too long ago, I opened my email and saw a message from a major television network. They were producing a series in partnership with the Southeastern Conference (SEC), a division of college football, and the US Army. Because of my background in both football and the military, they wanted me to participate. At first, I skimmed the details, assuming it would be another small opportunity. Then I saw my appearance fee: $100,000. Two games. A few lines on camera. First-class flights for my family.

There was a time when news like this would have sent my system into overdrive—excitement tangled with fear, my mind racing ahead, my body tensing, waiting for the other shoe to drop. This time, none of that happened.

The work I had been doing behind the scenes in my life—learning to recognize, reframe, and recenter—had created a new foundation in me. I was not pushing harder to make this happen. I was available for it because by creating inner safety, I created the spaciousness in my life to invite this type of opportunity in. I didn't need to manage the moment or brace for what came next. That's the deeper work of inner safety. It doesn't just keep us grounded when things fall apart. It creates space for aligned opportunities to come into our lives. It prepares us for abundance.

Life will always meet us at the level of inner safety we've

cultivated. Opportunities that are too big for our nervous system to carry will feel like burdens instead of gifts. Love that asks us to be fully seen will feel like a threat instead of a connection. Success that outpaces our inner safety will unexpectedly transform into another form of fear. But when safety is rooted within, that story shifts—we have real agency. We no longer have to sabotage or shrink the very things we've longed for. We can let them land, let them grow us, and let them expand what's possible.

This is the invitation—to stop chasing safety in the form of the external validation or risk-free opportunities—and to begin cultivating the kind of inner safety that allows you to receive it when life endows you with more.

A Gentle Invitation

This week, pay attention to moments when life feels too much—not just when it's hard, but also when it's too good. Notice the instant your system wants to rush, manage, numb, or shut down. That impulse is often the signal you've reached your capacity ceiling.

When you catch it, don't push through and don't check out. See it for what it is—an invitation to expand. Expansion rarely feels comfortable. It feels like exposure, responsibility, grief, vulnerability, or being more visible than you're used to. If you respond the same way you always have—pushing harder, checking out, trying to control the outcome—the ceiling stays in place, and you delay your growth.

So do one thing differently. Slow the moment by ten percent. Stay with what's happening in your body and name what's being stretched. Is it your tolerance for uncertainty, or your ability to be seen in a deeper way? Maybe it's your willingness to receive support and need other people, or it's your capacity to feel joy without expecting it to all come undone.

Repeated moments of staying present when your system wants to shut down are how inner safety is built. Each time you stay present, you teach your nervous system that it can carry more. Over time, the ceiling lifts, not because life asks less of you, but because you're able to hold more of what arrives.

Chapter Ten

THE DANCE OF DETACHMENT

The part of you that notices your anxiety is not moved by your anxiety.

— *Adyashanti*

Before trying "magic" mushrooms for the first time, I had heard enough stories about them to know they were unpredictable. I'd heard some people return from a trip and profess that it was the most profound experience of their lives. Others had sworn they would never touch them again after an overwhelming experience. At the time they came into my life, I was still the guy who thought meditation was a scam, so the idea that eating a handful of fungi in the middle of the woods could lead to enlightenment wasn't exactly convincing. Still, curiosity won—I wanted to experience it for myself.

For the first thirty minutes, I was mostly waiting around. The music was playing through big speakers, the trees stretched high above us, and I sat there, in the middle of the woods, like someone in a doctor's office—anticipating something but not quite sure what it was going to be. Then, without warning, the waiting ended. The music wasn't just surrounding me anymore—its rhythm moved through my chest until it felt like my body had dissolved into vibration. There was no line between where I ended and the sound began. I wasn't listening to music—I *was* the music. That was the doorway. Once I stepped through it, I realized I was no longer in control of where the experience was taking me. While I wasn't steering, I could feel myself being led gently and with compassion. The journey took me through moments that were strange, beautiful, and sometimes overwhelming, but eventually it carried me somewhere I wasn't expecting.

I landed in what felt like an infinite abyss of darkness. The abyss was nothing, but somehow it was also everything at the same time. I know how cliché that might sound, but it's true. There were no shapes, no colors, no sound, yet the darkness felt fully alive with something vast and unexplainable.

It was here, in the infinite abyss, that I encountered what I now understand to be my Big Self. This was not a figure or a voice booming from the clouds, but a presence that felt like the truest part of me. In that presence, I began to watch my entire life unfold like I was watching a movie reel. Moment after moment of childhood memories, football games, heartbreak, and ordinary mornings all flashed in front of me. I saw the victories I had chased and the failures I had feared. I saw the relationships I had clung to and the dreams I had tried in vain to control.

But here's what changed everything. As this movie of my life played, and I was sitting alongside the essence of my Big Self, I realized I was no longer in the film. I was the one watching it. The version of myself that I had always believed to be my true identity—the one who worked, strived, pushed, and excelled through each season of my life—was not the most authentic representation of who I am. The most authentic version of myself was the observer, calm and unaffected by the highs and lows of every scene. That night, I witnessed a part of myself that had always been present, even though I had never recognized its existence. Once I saw it, I could no longer ignore it.

Big Self/Small Self

What I uncovered in that moment was more than just a psychedelic revelation beneath the trees. It was the first time I confronted a truth that has influenced seekers in every culture: There are two versions of the self. There exists a small self that scrambles, strives, and panics when life takes an unexpected turn—and clings just as tightly to what's good out of the fear of losing it. There also exists the Big Self that observes everything unfold with a calm, unwavering steadiness.

I had spent most of my life living from the first one—the small self, which thrives on striving behaviors. It was the part of me that always wanted more, feared not being enough, and worked endlessly to stitch together some sense of control. The small self loves to keep score. It's the self that needs to win, clings to joy as if it might disappear, and resists pain as if it shouldn't exist. It's the self I built a career on, and the one that fueled my survival path. It's also the self that left me exhausted and drowning whenever life stopped cooperating with my plans.

Living this way feels like being tossed around by the waves. You're always gasping for air, crashing against the shore, never able to rest. The Big Self is more like the entire ocean itself. It doesn't thrash with every change in the wind. It's steady, deep, and able to hold and witness it all.

That day in the woods gave me a taste of life from the vantage point of the Big Self. I could see everything—my wins, my failures, the moments I wanted to relive, and the ones I wanted to forget—and none of it had power over me. The truer and more present me—my Big Self—wasn't in the movie of my life; it was the one observing the movie of my life.

It's important to note that the small self isn't evil or broken; it's simply incomplete. The small self is made up of the identity we cobble together in response to wounds, expectations, adaptations, and survival strategies. Most of us stay stuck in that limited perspective for so long that we assume it's all we are. But beneath that noise lies the Big Self.

This is clearly not unique to me. Almost every tradition identifies this same discovery. Buddhists refer to the small self as ego self, and the Big Self as anatta, or no self, representing the liberation that arises when one is no longer constrained by attachment. Hinduism refers to the individual self as jiva and the deeper self as Atman, the soul that is inseparable from God. In Sufi poetry, it is the Beloved who resides within. Christianity has long discussed the false self we create and the true self hidden with Christ in God. In the words of Thomas Merton, a writer that I admire, "Every one of us is shadowed by an illusory person, a false self . . . all sin begins with the assumption that my false self is the real self."

The words may differ, but the experience that framework describes is the same. Beneath the noise of our personalities and the stories we cling to lies a steadier ground. This deeper self isn't scrambling for approval or racing to keep control. When the storyline suddenly shifts, it remains steady. Rather than grasping or resisting, it simply notices.

Inner Spaciousness

I like to think of this Big Self as the observer. It's the part of you that notices what's happening without being swept away by it.

The observer sees your thoughts, emotions, and storylines play out but isn't fused to them. From this place, you're still in your life—loving, grieving, celebrating, stumbling—but you're not consumed by every rise and fall. This isn't detachment in the sense of numbing out or spiritually bypassing your problems. It's detachment in the sense that you're no longer bound by the context you find yourself in or the limitations of the material world.

Through the observer's practice of awareness, you began to see that you are not defined by your thoughts. You are simply the one who notices them. When you're able to recognize this shift, even in the ordinary moments like sitting in traffic, running late, or spiraling in anxiety, you realize you don't have to grip the wheel of your life so tightly because the true you is the one noticing these experiences. This awareness creates a healthy psychological distance between you and your life experience. From that distance, you are able to choose how to respond to anything that arises.

Learning how to connect to the observer within me, the Big Self, led me to discover an inner spaciousness I didn't know existed. Not the kind of spaciousness that comes from free time or an empty calendar, but something much more profound. Once I had cultivated this, even when life felt loud and chaotic, there was still space to breathe and to hold what was happening without being crushed by it.

Before we discover this kind of inner spaciousness, most of us move through life driven by our small self, stuck in survival mode. Everything feels tight. Even if our calendars aren't packed, our minds are racing, and our bodies carry the weight of an invisible pressure. We move through our lives holding our breath. Every setback feels like evidence of our failure. Every good moment slips away too quickly because we cling to it, terrified it won't last. We live fused to the storylines of our lives, as if the next scene has the power to either make us or break us.

That's how I lived for years. Always measuring, always gripping, always anxious that the whole thing might collapse if I stopped holding it together so tightly. Striving kept me confined in the small self, gasping for air like I was being tossed around at sea.

But when you tap into the spaciousness of the Big Self, the story shifts. Life doesn't stop being busy or painful or uncertain, but suddenly, there's enough room inside you for it. You still feel joy, but you don't need to grasp it so tightly, afraid you'll lose it. You still feel pain, but you're no longer drowning in it. You can move between both ends of the emotional spectrum without either one owning you. Inner spaciousness is what gives us back our lives.

This experience didn't just change how I moved through my everyday life, but it also challenged the faith I was handed as a boy and allowed me to discover it on my own.

I was raised in an evangelical Christian culture where I was taught, again and again, that my identity was in Christ. It was offered as an answer, not an experience. A phrase I was meant to believe in, not something I was taught how to embody. And the truth is, I still believe that today. What changed wasn't the belief itself, but how I understood it. I *believed* the words, but they weren't helping in the moments I met fear, pain, or uncertainty in my actual life.

I see Christ less as a distant historical figure I try to follow or emulate. I now experience him as an archetype of what a fully awake human life looks like: a living presence of love and awareness, the same presence I touch when I return to the observer, the Big Self. For me, what I've come to see is that the way Christ points us to is less about allegiance to a single religious figure in a particular religion, and more about an invitation into an awakened way of life that Jesus embodied and that can be recognized, in different forms, across several spiritual traditions. When Christ is understood this way, faith is no longer framed as competing truths, but as different expressions of the same love that connects us all. As a result, we become less guarded, less defensive, and more available to the love we claim to follow.

For years, I clung to the idea of being in Christ like a lifeline—something I reached for whenever I felt afraid or unworthy. What I've come to see is that this presence is not something to cling *to*—it's a place to live *from*. To live in Christ, for me, is to live from this deeper awareness, rather than from fear, striving, or self-protection.

This inner spaciousness has become my compass. When it's present, I feel grounded, moving through life's challenges and successes with ease. When it fades, it's a reminder I've drifted—and an invitation to return to the breath, the body, to the awareness that never leaves.

To get to this point, I wasn't constantly chasing another peak moment in the woods or depending on a heroic dose of mushrooms to feel whole again. What mattered to my progress was learning how to touch that same awareness in the middle of ordinary life—traffic jams, late nights with kids, deadlines, unmet expectations, all of it. Awareness itself has to be practiced. Without practice, it stays an inspiring memory. With practice, it becomes a way of being.

For me, the practice that opened the door was meditation.

Mediation—It's Not What You Think

When I sat down to meditate for the first time, I was still carrying the same playbook I had carried everywhere else—the playbook of striving. I thought success meant keeping my mind perfectly still. I thought the win would be measured by how long I could hold focus without drifting. Within seconds, my thoughts would wander, and I would feel the old voice rise up: *You're doing it wrong; you can't even get this right.* I walked away convinced meditation wasn't for me.

That misunderstanding is common because it mirrors the way we've been conditioned to live. We try to perfect even the act of letting go, but meditation doesn't work that way. The practice is about building your muscles of awareness and presence—not about erasing thought or being perfectly still.

Later on, when I heard spiritual teacher Tara Brach speak of meditation as "building the muscles of presence," everything clicked. For the first time, meditation made sense to me because of my background as an athlete. Training has never been about one flawless rep. It's about repetition, showing up, and strengthening. You can't always see your progress in the moment, but you know it will carry you when it counts. Meditation is no different. The reps are noticing the mind drift, and when you notice, bringing your awareness back to the breath, over and over again.

That shift changed everything about my relationship with meditation practice. At first, when I realized I had drifted, I felt frustrated. But now I saw it differently. Every moment of noticing was proof that the training was working. Because, when I noticed, I wasn't lost in the storyline anymore—I had stepped out of it. I was connected to the part of me that could observe it all, the Big Self.

As I built a personal practice of meditation, I began to see something I had missed my entire life. My suffering was never about the thoughts themselves but in how I clung to them. I tried to hold on to the pleasant ones, afraid they would slip away, and I fought against the painful ones, convinced they had no place. That endless tug-of-war was what left me restless and trapped.

Meditation was teaching me another way. Each time I sat down, I was practicing how to step outside the storyline I had always believed *was* me. Noticing the drifting and gently returning allowed me to meet my life with a new kind of awareness. What once felt like failure—my mind wandering—became evidence that the practice was working. Over time, I began to see I was no longer lost inside the scenes of my life, because I had built the muscles of awareness to observe them. I began to live in connection with my Big Self, the part of me that could hold joy and pain, gain and loss, without being consumed by either.

Resistance Creates Suffering

Not long ago, after years of rebuilding my life into something I could be proud of, I noticed my fear had changed shape. For so long, I was afraid of never reaching my destination, never arriving, never making it. However, after I had built something solid and meaningful for myself, the fear returned in a different form. Now it wasn't *What if I never get there?*, but *What if I lose it?*

Without realizing it, I was pouring an enormous amount of my limited energy into outrunning that fear. I clung tightly to my work, my relationships, even the joy I was finally allowing myself to feel, terrified it might all vanish. I wasn't just enjoying what I had built; I was guarding it. I was holding my life with the same amount of tension I had once chased it with. That is what clinging does: It drains the life out of the very things we love. Like trying to hold water in your hands, the tighter you squeeze, the faster it slips through your fingers.

To shift this experience, I didn't try to outwork or fix my fear. I stopped trying to outrun it and doubled down on a simple practice that allowed me to meet it. When the fear of losing what I had built would surface, usually out of nowhere, I didn't argue with it or avoid it. Regardless of where I was, or what I was doing, I would settle myself and gently repeat under my breath, *The part of me that is observing this fear is not moved by this fear.* I said it while walking, working, lying in bed at night, and while standing in line at Chick-fil-A.

At first, nothing really happened. But the more I practiced it, I started to notice that each time I sat back into the seat of awareness and connected with the Big Self—the observer—what once felt tight and restricted slowly began to feel more open and spacious. I wasn't trying to force calm. I was creating space around the fear instead of living inside of it.

This is when meditation gave me language for what was happening. The suffering didn't stem from the life I was living. It was coming from the grip I had on life. The more I tried to lock things down, the more anxious and fragile I felt. Once I recognized that pattern within myself, I began to notice how universally applicable it was: parents holding on to their children so tightly that no one can breathe, leaders gripping their success until it becomes suffocating, couples clinging to each other out of fear rather than love.

Life, however, is always moving in the opposite direction. The love language of the universe is expansion. It keeps inviting us into a deeper, wider, more spacious experience of ourselves and life itself. But the doorway to that expansion never opens through resistance or clinging; it opens through the dance of detachment. Only when our grip softens can life have breathing room to carry us somewhere new.

Striving mutates here. What once drove me to chase success eventually showed up again in a new disguise. I found myself clinging to what I had already built. It was the same energy, just wearing different clothes. Detachment revealed a different way forward—not grasping at the next win, not gripping the good I had, but loosening so life could keep moving through me.

This is the rhythm of unstriving. Not indifference, not walking away from what matters, but loosening the hold just enough so that love, creativity, and connection can breathe. It is trusting that joy can be received without clinging, and pain can be faced without resisting. It is learning that freedom isn't found in securing every outcome but in releasing the need to control them.

The entire journey of unstriving has been moving us toward a connection with the Big Self. The deeper presence within that notices what is happening but is never swallowed by it. Every return to awareness in meditation, every softening of the grip on the controls of life is a practice of this way of living. Slowly, steadily, a new center of gravity forms. This is not another strategy, not another playbook. It is the life that endures when striving loses its power. It is unstriving, alive and breathing in all of us.

A Gentle Invitation

So, wherever you find yourself right now—whether in the middle of something tender or something beautiful—pause. Step back enough to notice your surroundings and life's context—the scene that would be playing if you, too, were watching the movie of your life alongside your Big Self.

Ask yourself, *Where am I resisting what hurts, convinced it should not be here? Where am I clutching what feels good, afraid it might slip away?* Both keep life small and heavy. Both narrow the space where expansion is trying to happen.

There is a part of you that notices your fear, stress, sadness, or tension. That part of you is not shaken by what it notices. Fear can be loud, but the one who observes it is steady. That's the Big Self. It's already here. You don't have to earn it or achieve it. You just have to notice it.

Like any muscle, awareness gets stronger with practice and repetition. The simplest way to practice is meditation. If sitting for twenty minutes feels like too much, sit for two.

Once you find yourself sitting comfortably and

upright, bring your attention to your breath. Feel the inhale and the exhale. Notice the rise and fall of your chest. Keep your attention there. It might be two seconds or five, but your mind will wander. When you notice your mind has drifted, gently bring it back to the breath. Again. And again. And again.

This is how we engage in the dance of detachment. The beautiful part of this practice is that you can access it anytime, anyplace: in the car, the office, the bathroom, or even in line at Starbucks.

This practice serves as the foundation for a resilient form of detachment—equipping us for whatever lies ahead. Life will always continue to offer its invitations. The question is whether we will answer them with open hearts, prepared for what is unfolding.

Chapter Eleven

LETTING THE FOREST FIND YOU

"Stand still. The trees ahead and the bushes beside you
Are not lost. Wherever you are is called Here. . . . The
forest knows
Where you are. You must let it find you."

—David Wagoner, "Lost"

Nothing feels more disorienting than realizing the very tools that once kept you afloat no longer have power. You stop running, stop gripping, stop proving, and for a moment you're left suspended, wondering what comes next. This disorientation, while often uncomfortable, is the beginning of a deeper integration. By the time we arrive here, we have already begun to let go of old ways of surviving. We have faced pain instead of running from it. We have learned how to sit still and live with more ease. We have pulled the plug on the stories that held us back. We have discovered what it feels like to belong. We have begun to build a sense of safety inside ourselves and practiced dancing with detachment.

Yet the urge to return to the familiar sense of control, to push harder, to run faster, to think our way into clarity, is always present. That reflex will never fully disappear. But this is the point in the journey when a new way forward begins. Instead of trying to find the path by force, we must begin to allow the path to find us.

To me, this practice is best illustrated by the poem *Lost* by David Wagoner, who, inspired by the teachings of an old Native American elder story, wrote the following: *Stand still. . . . The forest knows / Where you are. You must let it find you.*

That kind of instruction sounds almost unthinkable in our loud and fast-paced world. When we feel lost, we don't stop moving—we charge forward, listening to another self-improvement podcast, writing another list to meet our goals, building another life plan. We try to force clarity with stimulation and distraction.

Maybe standing still even feels irresponsible. It feels like failure.

Which is why that line—*The forest knows / Where you are. You must let it find you*—caught my attention when I first read it, and I never stopped thinking about it. For as long as I can remember, this was the opposite of how I lived. Whenever I felt lost, I ran harder. Whenever I didn't know what to do, I made a plan. Whenever fear closed in, I pushed forward. I did everything I could to find my way out of feeling lost in the metaphorical forest of my life. It was all I knew. Wagoner's poem gave me a different instruction. Stop running. Stand still. Allow the forest to find you.

But standing still isn't as simple as it sounds. Often, there is something in us that refuses. It's the part that has been trained to keep moving at all costs, convinced our very survival depends on it.

The Loyal Soldiers

During World War II, a group of Japanese pilots was shot down and stranded on remote islands. Cut off from the outside world, they survived for years believing the war was still happening. When they were finally rescued and told the fighting had ended, many of them wanted to return to battle. Their entire identity was bound to the mission. They didn't know how to stop.

We who are learning to unstrive are not so different. Each of us carries what is known as loyal soldiers. These loyal soldiers are parts of us that came about early in life, carrying the singular mission of keeping us alive. They don't rest. They don't question orders. They are tireless in their devotion to survival.

For me, these soldiers took the shape of the performer, the perfectionist, the producer, and the guy addicted to exceptionalism. They carried me through locker rooms, into stadiums, and across stages—every space where I felt I had to prove my worth. Their sole mission was to win the war of my life, and they excelled at their job. But survival is not the same as living fully. I have come to realize that as long as these soldiers stay on duty, I cannot stand still. I cannot let the forest find me, because the soldiers will keep me running, fully convinced the war is still on.

The work we have done up to this point has changed that. By facing the pain we used to avoid, learning stillness, loosening our grip, and building a sense of safety within ourselves, we've grown. We are no longer the scared child who needs the soldiers to fight for our survival. The war is over. And if the war is over, the soldiers can finally go home.

That doesn't mean they'll vanish completely. Just like the soldiers returning to Japan after the war, they aren't cast aside or forgotten. They are honored, thanked, and reintegrated into the whole. Their loyalty remains, but their burden shifts. They're no longer responsible for running the show.

The question, then, is how? How do we thank these soldiers without discarding them? How do we release them from duty without turning against the very parts of us that once kept us alive? That became the work I had to learn—the work of honoring, integrating, and making space for something new.

Parts Work

I only began to grasp the significance of allowing the forest to find me with the help of a man named Peter. He was in his eighties, a seasoned Soulcraft guide, and although we had never met one another, his presence immediately felt akin to standing beside an ancient tree—solid, grounded, and steadfast.

One afternoon in my office, I told him about the journey I had been on. How much had changed. How much had softened. How, despite it all, I still felt constrained by an invisible ceiling. I still felt a profound need to understand my life, regain control, and figure out how to move things forward.

Peter nodded, like he had heard this before. Then he asked me to try something different. He told me to look around my office and find objects that represented the parts of me that had carried me this far—the soldiers who had fought for my survival.

My eyes landed on my autographed football from Roger Goodell welcoming me to the NFL, a framed *Sports Illustrated* article, my college jersey and helmet, and my West Point diploma. Each one was charged with a different story of me: the one addicted to being special, the producer who always had something to prove, the performer who couldn't stop striving, and the perfectionist who never allowed himself to miss the mark, whatever the cost.

Peter asked me to approach each object one by one, thank it

out loud, and then remove it from the room. It sounded simple enough, but by the second object, I was on my knees, sobbing. I hadn't realized how tightly I was still clinging to the man those objects represented. I hadn't realized how deeply tired those parts of me were—how ready they were to be dismissed.

When the last object was gone, the room felt stripped bare. What mattered wasn't the empty walls, but the shift that had taken place inside me. For the first time, I had turned toward my soldiers and told them the truth—the war was over. Their work had mattered, their loyalty had sustained me thus far, but now they could rest. They no longer needed to keep fighting like they once did. In this simple but profound ceremony, I was honoring, thanking, and welcoming home the loyal soldiers who were once so dedicated to the fight. Their devotion remained, but their burden had changed.

That day in my office was not therapy. It was a ritual. Through this practice, space opened in me. It felt unfamiliar but alive—a clearing where something new could finally come through.

We each carry our own versions of those objects. They may not look like jerseys or diplomas, but you'll know them when you feel like you can't lose them without losing yourself.

What I began to see is that those instincts to prove, perform, or perfect myself just to stay safe weren't flaws. They were my soldiers still on duty. They were still fighting a war that had already ended. Until they are seen, honored, and told the truth that the war is over, they will keep you running. They will not let you stand still long enough for the forest to find you.

When the loyal soldiers finally set down their weapons, another way of living becomes possible. The space they leave behind is not empty; it's fertile. And what emerges from that clearing is not another plan or strategy, but the part of us that has been waiting to be seen.

The Wild Child

In depth psychology, this part of us is sometimes called the Wild Child. Robert Bly referred to it as an ancient Gnostic secret, which states that when you were born, your mother simultaneously gave birth to a wild twin. Unlike you, this wild twin was hurled out the window and forced to survive on its own in some far-off place. What Bly was pointing to is a split that happens early in life. As we learn to be accepted, productive, and praised, we start to shape ourselves around what is rewarded. Parts of our original nature are set aside. These parts weren't set aside because they are wrong, but because they simply didn't fit the mold of expectation. Over time, that exiled part of us doesn't disappear. It waits for our reunion, but the longer it waits, the more our lives become shaped by adaptation rather than authenticity. Its absence is often felt years later as a sense that something is missing in our lives—regardless of how much we accomplish. The work of becoming whole, Bly said, is to make our way back to that exiled part of ourselves to reclaim the parts we abandoned in exchange for the approval of others and a false sense of belonging.

The Wild Child is the untamed, vital, original self that existed before the world taught us to shrink ourselves. It is the instinctual, adventurous self that carries our deepest sense of purpose. This part doesn't need to seek out peak experiences to feel alive, but it lives in the raw, ordinary moments of life and feels fully alive. Mud between your toes, ocean waves crashing against your body, the sun on your face, while the blackbirds sing—it is fully present for these moments, and they are, in and of themselves, enough. This is often the part of us that is so quickly dismissed, pushed aside in favor of productivity and responsibility. Yet this is our primal wildness that knows how to feel, how to belong to the earth, and how to be satisfied without needing life to look any other way. It is the essence of aliveness.

This Wild Child is what we have been striving for all along. All our efforts—striving, proving, producing, and perfecting—carry the hope that one day we will truly feel alive, seen, and safe enough to express our authentic selves. We've trained other aspects of ourselves to obtain those things on our behalf. Those parts worked. They bought time and ensured our safety. But we were unaware that their success could undermine the very thing we desired. When the clearing opens and the Wild

Child returns, we realize that the life we believed was beyond us has been within us all along.

The purpose of all the work we've undertaken so far in this journey has been to confront the pain, release our grip, and cultivate a sense of safety within. All of it was to prepare for the return of what had been abandoned.

I brought this awareness with me into the forest as I participated in the weeklong Soulcraft intensive I mentioned earlier. I didn't go with the intention of seeking out an alternative plan for my life. I went because I felt there was something within me that could only be discovered in the wilderness. The issue was that I had always maintained an uneasy relationship with the wild. From afar, I appreciated its beauty, but upon closer inspection, its chaos left me feeling unsettled. The intertwining roots, the buzzing of insects, and the palpable vibrancy stirred a sense of unease in me. It was only later that I recognized my attitude toward the forest reflected my attitude toward my own wild nature. My fear of the wilderness outside mirrored my fear of the wilderness within.

For the first few days, nothing seemed to break open. I wandered the land and gave myself over to small ceremonies in an attempt to get out of my head and into my body. One day, I officiated a wedding with the trees, as if to ritualize the longing I carried for a deeper union with life itself. Another day, I held a funeral for a season of my life that was passing, my way of acknowledging what had died and could not return. These gestures mattered. They gave form to what I was feeling inside. But still, nothing seemed to break me open. I felt like I was circling something I couldn't quite touch. The ache remained.

While I didn't know it at the time, I was being primed. Something was waking up inside of me. My expectations were being hollowed out, making space for something wild, whole, and true to find me.

On the second-to-last night of the intensive, we were invited to take part in a trance dance ceremony. I had never done anything like it before. When I heard that we'd be painting our faces, dressing in ceremonial clothes, and dancing around a fire for ninety minutes, everything in me wanted to say, "Yeah, not happening." Thankfully, participation wasn't mandatory. We were told we could simply hold space on the outer edges of the fire for those who felt called to the dance. That was my plan.

Later that night, with my face painted like a warrior, I stood at the edge of the circle watching others move barefoot through the dirt, their bodies giving themselves over to the rhythm of the drums. I had no intention of joining. I told myself I was there, that I was participating—but I wasn't. I was still standing at the margins, letting life happen around me while I stayed safely in the role of bystander. But the longer I stood there, the more I felt something stirring in me, a pull that had no words and over which I had no control.

Halfway through the dance, a force rose up from the ground beneath me. It felt primal and unfamiliar, but at the same time deeply known, as if it had always been there, hiding and in waiting. It moved through me like an electrical current, shaking me loose from my thoughts and judgment. My body bent at the waist, arms hanging limp at my sides, and I let the music take me. I didn't try to lead or understand—I just let it happen. One moment I was a spectator, and the next I was moving into the firelight. My feet hit the dirt, my body found the rhythm, and suddenly I was no longer watching the dance—I was in it.

Later, I realized how much that moment mirrored the rest of my life. For years, I had lived at the edges, close enough to feel the heat but not willing to risk the flames. I had worked hard, performed well, and played my roles. I had even done plenty of inner work. But in some deeper way, I had stayed just outside the circle of my own life. And this is where so many of us find ourselves. We tell ourselves we're in the dance because we're near the fire—sending the emails, checking the boxes, saying the right things. But deep down, we know we're only circling the edges. We intrinsically know the difference between watching and risking. The edges are safer, but they are also lonelier. They can never offer us the fire's heat, which burns away pretense and leaves only what is real and most alive.

That night, when I stepped in, it was not just about a trance dance. It was about moving from the edges into the center for myself. I was no longer looking on. I was in the fire, in the dirt, and in my body, finally letting the rhythm move me.

When the drums softened and the circle began to slow, I lay on the ground. My chest rose and fell with heavy breaths, and the dirt pressed cool against my back. I stayed there for a long time, letting the silence spread through me. In that stillness, I sensed something I hadn't felt since I was a child. It was wild and alive. My body knew it before my mind did.

A force had been waiting beneath the surface, patient and untamed, and moved through me. The ache I had carried for so long took shape, and I recognized it as the Wild Child I had left behind. I didn't really understand what it meant, but I knew I didn't need to figure it out. I only needed to notice that what had been exiled was present again; I could feel it breathing with me in the dirt.

When the Forest Found Me

The next morning, I walked back into the woods for my final wander before heading home. Based on my experience the previous night, I decided to wander south, the direction that belongs to the Wild Child in Soulcraft tradition. With each step I took, something felt different. It was like the earth itself was pulling me in deeper. Whatever I had touched during the trance dance was not finished with me.

Out of curiosity, I decided to put the Wild Child on, almost like slipping into a costume, to see what would happen if I gave him room to speak. I had spent years avoiding and ignoring the Wild Child, so I wanted to give him space to move in an attempt to get to know him. Once again, I stripped down naked, mixed water with dirt, smeared it over my face and body, and began to move through the woods. First, the growl came, low in my chest, then the grunts and snarling. Before long, my body was coursing with the same primal energy I had felt the night before. I was wild, untamed, and fully alive.

As I moved, a strange awareness rose in me. It felt like I was hunting something, though I didn't know what at first. With each step, it became clearer. I was hunting the little boy in me who was still afraid of this untamed force. The boy who had been told to be quiet, to sit still, to behave. The boy who once ran through the woods but traded his howl for applause. The boy who trembled inside me every time I was about to say something true. For years, he had been guarded by loyal soldiers, but now he stood fully exposed. That's who I was after.

So, I ran through the woods. I was out of my head and fully in my body. I don't know how long I moved, only that time seemed to dissolve. Eventually, I stumbled into a small clearing. In the center stood a massive dead tree stump covered in moss, vines, and weeds. It looked almost monstrous—twisted and grotesque—but it was still beautiful in its own way. I recognized it as a symbol of the Wild Child in me, standing there in plain sight.

I put my clothes back on and sat in front of the stump. With a few deep breaths, I connected to the trembling little boy inside me, and asked: *Why are you chasing me? Why are you trying to hurt me?*

In the tension and silence of the unanswered question, I opened my journal and let my hand move across the page. In that space, the Wild One finally answered:

I am not here to harm you. I am here to give you back what you have forgotten. I am here to place your howl back in your throat, to return your courage to your chest, to restore the joy that no applause can buy. I am not your enemy. I am your freedom. I am the part of you that was never tamed, never traded, never lost—only waiting for you to remember.

When the Wild Child finally met the little boy in me, I began to weep. It was a reunion of the pieces of myself that had been split apart. The little boy no longer needed to fear the Wild Child, and the Wild Child no longer needed to live in exile. In their meeting, something long-buried surfaced again. My vitality, my original voice, the essence of who I am, my innate sense of wholeness—all of it came rushing back. For the first time, I wasn't chasing life with my head. I was inhabiting it with my body.

Sitting there, in the middle of the woods, I leaned up against the tree stump to let my head catch up to what my heart was feeling. I looked down and saw an earthworm come up from the ground, crawl over my hand, and then press down into the soil again.

And I knew. The forest was speaking back.

The worm wasn't just a worm. It was a witness. Like the gift our ancestors once gave to those returning from rites of passage, the forest was offering me a new name. One that carried both weight and direction. A name that wasn't about achievement or status, but about essence.

"*You are Earthworm,*" the forest said. "*You move where others refuse to look. What has been discarded, you make fertile. What has been hardened, you soften. You are the bridge between what has been lost and what will grow again. Your journey through the dark is what makes new life possible for others. You make space for new roots to take hold and for what's next to rise.*"

I sat in silence and continued to weep.

The forest found me.

And here's the thing—life is always trying to get the heart's attention. It's through these moments that we are able to wake up something we already know but may have forgotten. The worm reminded me of the deeper work I was born to do—not the work chasing greater success—but the work of facilitating transformation, a deeper work that connected to my soul purpose.

Life has ways of doing this for all of us. A bird lingers too long on the branch, and you realize you've also been staying in a place you've outgrown, restless for change. A lyric breaks you open, and you remember you're still someone who feels deeply, even if you've gone numb. A stranger's words catch you off guard, revealing a truth you've been avoiding or a dream you still carry. These ordinary moments remind us of what's still alive in us.

The question was never whether life speaks to us. The question is whether we will slow down long enough to hear what it's saying.

A New Way Forward

What I experienced in the forest was neither about achievement nor healing as I had previously defined them. It was about something deeper—it was about union. The frightened little boy, who struggled to fully embrace his life, and the Wild Child, who defiantly refused to stay exiled, finally encountered each other, and from their meeting, something complete emerged.

This is the ultimate goal that unstriving has been guiding us toward all along. Not a plan or a brighter future to pursue, but a way of living that shifts from searching for a better life to fully embodying the one we're already living. It encourages us to face the ache we bear not as an issue to be resolved, but as a call to reconnect with what has been patiently waiting within us all along.

This is an invitation for all of us. We must stop exhausting ourselves in the endless striving in hopes that one day it will be enough. We must begin trusting that the life we are hunting down can be found inside us. We must begin to live in our bodies, not our minds. Only then can we feel the full scope of vitality that striving could never deliver. Only then can we trust our voice, feel our wholeness, and discover, joyfully, that the life we long for has already begun.

A Gentle Invitation

Take a few minutes to move through your house or office. Find different objects that represent a loyal soldier inside you. It might be a trophy that represents the performer, a planner that carries the perfectionist, or a laptop that represents the producer in you—the one who always responds and keeps things moving forward.

Choose one item and place it in front of you. Take a moment to notice what it has helped you do and what it has protected you from. If it feels right, speak to it. If speaking feels uncomfortable, write a short letter instead. Let this loyal soldier know you see their effort.

For example, you might choose your laptop. It represents the producer in you, the part that learned early on that being useful meant being safe. You don't tell it to shut down or go away. You thank it for what it's done and the opportunities it created. Then you say something like, *I still need you, just not all the time. You don't have to be on duty every moment for me to be okay.*

The work doesn't disappear, and the emails still need to be answered. What changes is the urgency and sense that everything depends on this part never letting up. The loyal soldier doesn't leave, but it learns it doesn't have to lead anymore. It can finally rest—and so can you.

Chapter Twelve

FLOWING WITH THE RIVER

There is no rushing a river. When you go there, you go at the pace of water, and that pace ties you into a flow that is older than life on this planet. Acceptance of that pace, even for a day, changes us, reminds us of other rhythms beyond the sound of our own heartbeats.

— Jeff Rennicke

It's easy to imagine transformation as this big thing that happens when we abandon one life and choose to walk toward another. Sometimes transformation does look like that—dramatic and instantaneous—like when we leave a job or end a relationship. But the reality is that even through these changes, most of life remains the same. The bills still come due. The inbox still fills. The same repetitive conversations and mundane responsibilities wait for us. What has shifted is not the landscape, but the one who walks through it.

Similarly, the unstriving journey doesn't necessarily hand you a different world—it offers you a different way of being in *your* world. The self that once survived through force, control, and endless pushing is invited to soften into something steadier, truer, and more whole. You may carry the same life, but it rests differently on your shoulders. And that is no small thing because when the way you carry your life changes, the way life feels while you're living it changes. We no longer rush the river—we learn to move with it. We no longer measure success by how much we can do, but by how good we feel while doing it.

This is when the work of transformation moves beyond unstriving. It shifts from undoing to living. The question now is how to move forward, living from this new place. How to meet challenges with equanimity, pursue what we truly value, and build a future where we can thrive. How to make choices not from exhaustion, but from a place of rest—the inner rest that comes from no longer being at war with your own life.

And when you move from that rest, you may find that life begins to meet you differently. Perhaps doors you once had to force open will seem to begin to open on their own. Or, maybe, the right people will surprisingly appear in your life at the right time. This is what can happen after the forest finds you—the ease of a life in alignment. The current you once fought against now carries you. Your work is no longer to make things happen, but to let yourself be met by what is already happening.

Rediscovering Rest

Years ago, I put a single word at the top of my Instagram profile: Rest. I didn't know why at the time. I couldn't explain it. Looking back, I can see how prophetic it was. My life was already moving me toward that simple discovery. What I longed for wasn't escape from pressure, but a version of inner rest that would truly sustain me through unfinished work and unpredictable days.

We live in a culture that has reduced rest to leisure: a weekend at the beach or a lazy Sunday on the couch. Rest is sold to us as escape—something you schedule when you can't keep going anymore, or something you earn only after the work is done. But that idea of rest is superficial and temporary. It soothes for a moment, but any benefit disappears as soon as life's demands return. It doesn't matter how much external time you take off when you're still internally on.

I'd like to invite us to engage in a deeper rest—not an intermission from life, but the new posture we live from. This kind of reset isn't about doing less, but it's about no longer living in constant internal tension. It's the difference between moving through your days feeling pressured and strained and moving through them with a sense of steadiness. From that place, effort becomes more sustainable, and ambition no longer feels frantic.

The unstriving journey has always been about this deeper form of rest. At some point, the old engine had to die—the one powered by fear, control, and survival. I fought that death for years. It felt like losing my edge. But when it finally gave out, I discovered that my ambition didn't vanish. Desire didn't fade. What burned away was the frantic energy I mistook for drive, and in its place was a steadier flame. Not less ambition, but ambition unchained from fear.

This is an invitation to rest. Not to abandon your vision of the future or lower your sights for success, but to approach them differently. Rest doesn't eliminate responsibility, but it alters how that responsibility weighs on your shoulders. It doesn't silence the drive to create, but it frees creation from the burden of survival. This is how we build something worth creating without losing our soul in the process.

The implications extend beyond us as individuals. We live in systems that are built on exhaustion—workplaces that reward burnout, economies that thrive on speed, and identities propped up by the need for validation. A culture that keeps us restless is a culture that keeps us compliant. To rediscover rest is not only a personal liberation but also reshapes the conditions we collectively live and work within. When we stop fueling ourselves with fear, we cease to feed the very machinery that maintains fear's power.

Rest ripples outward. A rested leader creates space for others to breathe. A rested parent provides their children with a model of wholeness. A rested creator makes work that nourishes rather than drains. This is why the unstriving journey matters. It is not just about you finding your center. It is about reimagining what becomes possible when a life, a family, or even an organization is anchored by that center.

Mystics across many cultures have always had language for this. Taoism calls it wu wei—effortless action. Not the absence of effort, but the absence of resistance. A way of moving where nothing is forced, yet nothing is left undone. This is the deeper participation we are invited into by the unstriving journey. For when your life begins to move from a place of rest, you will discover that the current is already carrying you. The invitation is to stop thrashing harder and be met by what is already happening.

Aikido

I first encountered aikido during a period when I was struggling to find a new direction for my life. I had already started the process of unstriving. My old ways of force and control were breaking down, but I still lacked an understanding of what it meant to live from this new foundation. Although I have never practiced it, aikido provided me with a vocabulary for the feelings I couldn't yet articulate. It illustrated what it means to approach life with presence rather than force.

Aikido is a Japanese martial art and meditation practice founded by Morihei Ueshiba, who is remembered as O Sensei, the Great Teacher. What sets it apart from other martial arts is its relationship to force. This practice is not about overpowering an opponent or dominating a situation. It is about meeting energy as it is, redirecting it, and resolving conflict through presence rather than aggression. In aikido, you don't meet tension with more tension. You meet it with awareness and presence. You don't try to win by controlling the situation—rather, you move with it.

This theory of force is where we find our value. Many of us understand how to persevere or succumb to pressure. However, many of us struggle to remain present during times of tension and allow a new path forward to unfold. When we relate to tension this way, it reshapes how we approach hard conversations, major decisions, and moments of loss.

Ultimately, the essence of the unstriving journey is to cease living in opposition to life and, instead, to flow with it. Reframe your reactions from fear or control and start responding from a position of alignment. Regardless of whether it's a difficult conversation, an unexpected transition, or an emotion you were never taught to manage, the key to moving forward lies not in overpowering these experiences, but in embracing them differently. Aikido returns us to the natural order not by force, but by allowing something deeper to lead. As Wendy Palmer writes in *The Intuitive Body*, "the capacity to be, without doing, is a particularly exquisite experience in life as we now accept life exactly how it is."

For so long, we have only lived for the doing, the fixing, and the striving. But now we are learning to live from a deeper source. Palmer names this deeper source as the feminine. Not gender, but energy. The feminine energy is the spaciousness from which action arises. It is the stillness beneath movement, the emptiness from which clarity emerges. It is the part of us that knows how to hold, receive, listen, and allow. And in a culture obsessed with performance and productivity, this kind of presence is often dismissed as weakness.

But there is nothing weak about stillness. It requires strength to accept things as they are rather than hastily trying to change them. It requires courage to sit in tension without seeking to control it. It takes trust to let life unfold without forcing an outcome. Palmer reminds us that "laziness is not inaction, but inattention." Our issue is not that we've done too little, but that we've done too much from a place of disconnection.

For most of us, the masculine has been the dominant mode of movement. We've been trained to act, assert, and push forward with certainty. There is beauty in that. But when the masculine operates without the feminine, it loses its spaciousness and its center. Eventually, it cuts itself off from the wisdom that only the feminine can bring. Palmer writes, "the masculine intention, the desire to know, often overlays the feminine, the not knowing, the mystery of life. The result is that the feminine aspect is cut short or cut off altogether. A whole part of ourselves is lost, buried under our knowledge."

This is something many of us have experienced without knowing how to articulate it. We have experienced only a fraction of life, lacking the aspect of ourselves that doesn't seek to control and instead understands how to wait, feel, and listen. The aspect that allows one to trust in the unfolding of life. In that absence, we have mistakenly interpreted doing more as the solution to the dissatisfaction we experience within.

Aikido invites us back into a right relationship with our energies. It shows us that when we stop resisting, we stop feeding what we resist. It calls us into the sacred dance of masculine and feminine, where movement arises from stillness. Force is no longer the opposite of flow, but its partner. We still act, but our action is now rooted in presence, not performance, and alignment, not urgency.

The shift is subtle but profound. The masculine energy no longer chases a future that might one day make us safe. It moves us more deeply into the reality that's already here. And when the masculine and feminine move together, everything changes. We are no longer fighting the river of life. We are simply in it.

Power Over vs. Power With

For most of our lives, we've been trained to engage the world through a strategy of *power over*. This is the posture of striving, control, and domination. It tells us that life is something to conquer, that success is something to win, and that safety can only be secured by getting ahead of others. This way of moving has been so normalized that we hardly question it. It drives our economies, our workplaces, even our families. But its fuel is fear. And fear eventually exhausts us.

When we learn to live differently, that entire relationship with power begins to shift, and we begin to discover an alternative strategy: *power with*. Instead of treating life as an opponent to outmaneuver, we learn to participate with it. Instead of trying to bend everything to our will, we begin to move with what is already moving. Presence opens a different kind of strength.

It's the difference between rowing and sailing. Power over is like gripping the oars, straining with every muscle, convinced that if you stop rowing, you'll lose everything you've gained. Power with is like learning to raise the sail. You still guide the boat, but you do it in partnership with the wind. The strength is no longer yours alone. You'll move farther and with less exhaustion, not because you forced harder, but because you allowed yourself to be carried by what was already there.

Power with is not a form of passivity. It doesn't mean surrendering your agency or shrinking your vision. It means living awake to the fact that life itself is imbued with energy, intelligence, and possibility—and when we align ourselves with those ever-present forces, we can be carried farther than control could ever take us. We stop asking, "How can I make this happen?" and start asking, "How can I join what is already happening here?"

That small difference changes everything. Power over leaves us isolated, endlessly competing, and afraid to let go. Power with draws us into deeper relationships—with ourselves, with others, and with the larger currents of life. In that spaciousness, our ambition becomes cleaner. Our leadership becomes more human. Our relationships stop being measured by control and start being shaped by trust.

We see it everywhere. A leader who shifts from power over to power with resists the urge to control a meeting when things feel uncertain and instead, staying present long enough for others to think, speak, and contribute in ways they wouldn't under pressure. A parent who shifts from power over to power with notices the impulse to intimidate or correct and chooses connection over compliance—even when it would be faster to enforce control. A team that makes this shift stops competing internally for credit and begins sharing responsibility, trusting that alignment creates better outcomes than dominance ever could.

If we widen the lens, we begin to see what could change in our culture. For generations, societies have been built on power over—nations competing for dominance, economies thriving on extraction, and workplaces rewarding burnout. The result is the same as in our personal lives—exhaustion, disconnection, division. But imagine what might unfold if power with began to bloom as the dominant ideology. Imagine workplaces built on cooperation instead of fear, economies oriented toward sustainability instead of depletion, politics grounded in shared humanity rather than endless rivalry. The shift that begins in us has the power to ripple outward into everything we touch.

What we have to remember is that culture is not an abstract machine operating independently of us. It is the accumulation of how we each choose to live. Every time you shift from control to collaboration, from domination to trust, you are tilting the scale of power in culture. You are proving that another way is possible. What starts in you does not end in you.

The river is moving. The current is carrying you. The wind is blowing. The question is no longer how hard you can row, but whether you are willing to raise the sail. Raising the sail is not so abstract. It is the daily choice to loosen your grip on control and orient yourself to what is already moving. It means listening before reacting. It's discerning the opportunity of disruption instead of fighting it. It's leaning into collaboration when you used to default to domination.

Raising the sail means you are still steering, still moving forward, but you are no longer exhausting yourself to create the wind. You are partnering with it—harnessing it.

Discipline Reborn

Whenever I discuss the concept of unstriving, a natural question follows: What happens to discipline? What happens to willpower, drive, and determination? For many of us, these have been the tools that carried us through life. Without them, it can feel like we'll drift into complacency. But what actually happens when we learn to unstrive is not the loss of discipline, but its transformation—from force into devotion.

The word *discipline* comes from the same root word as *disciple*. At its core, a disciple is not someone who obeys rules without question, but a learner, a student, an apprentice. To be disciplined is to apprentice yourself to a way of being. It is devotion to something that shapes you. Over time, culture—and often religion—has flattened the meaning of this word into one of conformity and control. Discipline has become about punishment, obedience, and rigidity. That distortion has left us with the belief that discipline is something harsh we must impose on ourselves, rather than a path we can choose to walk in life. The original meaning was never domination; it was devotion.

The culture of striving turned discipline into a whip. It demanded we drive ourselves harder, grip tighter, and never stop pushing. That kind of discipline exhausts us because it is fueled by fear—the fear of not being enough, of being left behind, of losing our worth if we let go. But when discipline is reborn through unstriving, it no longer serves fear. It serves alignment.

To live with discipline under this framework is to apprentice yourself to the way of wholeness. It is to keep returning to the stable center you have discovered within you, letting your daily practices, rhythms, and choices emerge from that ground. This kind of discipline doesn't shrink your freedom. It secures it. It creates the container where desire can safely surface without being drowned out by fear responses.

And desire will surface. Not the frantic cravings of ego or the endless "shoulds" that weigh us down, but a more honest desire that rises from this center. It is the energy of life itself, moving through us, drawing us forward.

When discipline is fueled by fear, desire is distorted. It comes out tangled in cravings, comparisons, and a list of "shoulds." But when discipline keeps us aligned with our center, desire is no longer scattered or suspect. It becomes clean, uncluttered by external messaging. It becomes trustworthy. When desire is trustworthy, it can become the compass for how we live.

This is not a new discovery. Benedict of Nursia, a sixth-century monk often regarded as the father of Western monasticism, authored what has become known as *The Rule of St. Benedict.* He emphasizes rhythm and the organization of daily life around prayer, work, study, and rest, rather than focusing on punishment, so that devotion can be sustained over a lifetime. Taoist literature speaks of walking in harmony with the Tao, where discipline is the steady return to flow rather than the fight against it.

And this is what it means for us: Discipline reborn does not diminish our ambition, drive, or determination—it purifies and deepens them. It signifies that we no longer need to push ourselves forward out of fear of failure or being left behind. Instead, we dedicate ourselves to what we recognize as life-affirming. Our daily rhythms aren't frantic attempts to control everything, but steady practices that keep us aligned with the center. Desire is no longer suspect but becomes a flame we can trust to guide us. Drive still burns. Willpower still matters. But now they move in the right direction, flowing from alignment rather than fear. This looks like rising early to create space for what matters most before the day demands your full attention. It looks like saying no to the "shoulds" that scatter your energy so that you're available to say yes to what you truly want. It looks like holding steady rhythms that free you to create, love, and lead without burning out. We trust that when we return to the center, the center will hold.

Trusting the Emergence

I've come to believe that the most meaningful parts of life—the moments that change us, the work that calls us, the versions of ourselves we've never met but know we're becoming—don't arrive because we force them into existence. They arrive because we allow them to.

When Kara was in labor with our second child, Rune, time lost all meaning for us. For sixty-three hours, her body would tighten with bone-deep contractions, every muscle straining, and then slowly loosen as the pain gave way to a moment of release. Waves rising and falling. Expansion and contraction. Pressure and pause. The rhythm of birth itself.

By the time we reached the hospital, Kara's body was

trembling with exhaustion, but she stayed open, surrendering in a way that was beyond her mind's control. I watched her meet each surge, sometimes tensing through it, sometimes softening into it, until she was no longer trying to control what was happening. Her body had given itself over to the rhythm of birth—the rise, the peak, the release.

And then, at the very edge of new life, our doctor leaned close, placed a steady hand on Kara's arm, and spoke with the softest, most grounded voice: "*The best births are the ones that are allowed. And you're doing it, sweetie.*"

Those words have never left me. They didn't just describe what was happening in that delivery room. They named everything I've spent a lifetime trying to learn about transformation, emergence, and the idea that becoming doesn't happen through willpower but through surrender. That's what I wanted: the kind of life we don't control but make space for.

This has been the thread of our entire journey together. We've loosened our grip on striving. We've discovered rest as the posture behind everything. We've practiced moving with energy instead of against it. We've shifted from power over to power with. We've watched discipline be reborn as devotion, aligning us with the center that holds. All of it has been leading us here to trust what wants to emerge.

Emergence is the rising of what has been forming beneath the surface, often long before we can see it. It is not manufactured by force or achieved by willpower. It is what happens when we create space, stay with the tension, and trust the hidden work of life. Just as a seed pushes through the soil when the season is right, or a child is born after months of unseen growth, emergence is the becoming that unfolds when conditions allow it. It rarely looks neat. It rarely follows our plans. But it is the way something true takes shape—not because we controlled it, but because we allowed it.

The world tells us to push harder, to rush, to manufacture results. But we have learned another way. We've let old strategies die, cleared rubble from outdated identities, and followed the ache instead of outrunning it. We've made space, and now something new is ready to rise.

This is not a shinier version of you to impress the world. It is a deeper truth that has been waiting beneath the noise. It asks for patience, radical acceptance, and the courage to stay open even when nothing feels certain. It asks you to trust that the center will hold.

I believe there is more inside us than we have yet found words for. Parts of us are waiting beneath the noise, holding a life we haven't yet lived. When we stop forcing and contriving, when we allow instead of control, those parts begin to rise. They surface not as something we can manufacture, but as something we get to meet. So, take a deep breath. Feel the ground beneath you. Trust what is moving through you. Because the best births, the ones that bring forth something more expansive and beautiful than we could ever imagine, aren't the ones we force. They're the ones we allow.

And you're doing it, sweetie.

A Gentle Invitation

Shifting from power over to power with takes time and patience. For the next week, use this short writing practice once a day.

1. Identify where you are still using power over. Answer these two questions as honestly as you can:
   - Where in my life am I trying to force progress right now?
   - What am I afraid will happen if I stop pushing?
2. Next, name the cost of that strategy.
   - In one to two sentences, write what this forcing is costing you. Maybe it's your energy, your presence, your peace, or even your relationships.
3. Create an *if-then* plan. When you notice yourself in a power over position, what can you do to shift out of it?
   - *If* you notice the urge to force an outcome, *then* pause and ask, "What would it look like to return to my center here instead of pressing in harder?"

Conclusion

BEGINNING AGAIN

And the end of all our exploring will be to arrive where we started and know the place for the first time.

T. S. Eliot

You may have set out on your unstriving journey thinking you needed to find a new life, but what you have found instead is a new way of living the one already in front of you. This journey has never been about escaping the life you have—it has been about meeting it differently. The place you began is the place you now return to, only now it is no longer ordinary—it is alive with meaning you couldn't see before.

Now comes the hardest and most beautiful part—beginning again.

Beginning again means forgetting. You will fall back into striving. You will grip too hard. You will try to row harder when the headwinds are already blowing. That's okay. The gift of beginning again is that there is no failure—only the next chance to return. Each sunrise is another threshold, each breath another chance to loosen your grip and step back into the flow of life that is already carrying you.

So, when Monday starts with unexpected disruptions and the panic hits, and you feel yourself slipping back into clinging tighter, working longer, and trying to outperform the discomfort instead of feeling it, begin again. When you notice yourself measuring your worth by how much you can produce or how polished you sound, and you catch yourself editing your words, your tone, or your personality in real time so you stay impressive, begin again. When you have a quiet moment to yourself and instead of resting, you reach for your phone, your to-do list, or your next goal because slowing down feels irresponsible and stillness feels unsafe, begin again. Each moment is an invitation to return. To stop forcing your life and choose to ground yourself in the fertile soil you've uncovered instead of tumbling around the barren lands of your life of striving.

As I've been writing this book, my speaking business has slowed down tremendously. Writing a book takes an incredible amount of time and energy, and with still being a full-time dad and husband, there hasn't been much time to focus on growing that side of my work. With speaking being our main source of income, you can maybe imagine the stress that created. So, when opportunities did come up, I started to realize how much I needed them to work out.

Things were looking good when I had four speaking engagements in my pipeline that felt like sure things. Money was tight, and this felt like exactly what we needed. Then, in the span of one day, all four speaking engagements fell apart for different reasons. Almost immediately, my thoughts started to race ahead of my life. A wave of panic hit, and I jumped into figure-it-out mode.

For the next few weeks, I doubled down on what has worked for years—exerting more effort, deploying more willpower, and striving harder. But it didn't take long for me to see and feel that the more I tried to strive ahead of the tension, the more I felt pulled into it. And the more I felt pulled into it, the more that old familiar feeling returned—soul tired. In my attempt to solve my problem through more striving, I was reinforcing it.

This leaked into every aspect of my life. It affected how I was showing up as a husband, father, and friend. I was short with my family, distracted with my friends, and self-critical of myself. My patience was thin, my presence was absent, and my joy was gone.

One afternoon on a walk, it hit me how absurd it was that I was writing a book titled *Unstriving* while my days were built around endlessly striving. I didn't need a new strategy; I needed to stop pretending I didn't see what I was doing and choose to live the message. Later that day, instead of opening my laptop in an attempt to make my life happen, I grabbed a notebook and sketched out plans for a small fire pit in our backyard. This was an idea I'd been carrying around for months, but I constantly dismissed it as unnecessary and unproductive. It was the kind of thing that doesn't necessarily move the needle, so it's what you do after life settles down, not when it's full of uncertainty. But it was what I really wanted to do. So, the next day I started the work.

I measured a circle, dug up the grass, ordered the gravel, and bought some stones. For the next week, my hands stayed dirty, but my computer remained closed. While I was bringing it all together, my mind kept driving to the same place—money. Initially, I couldn't shake the feeling that I was screwing up by not being at my desk and working harder. But instead of operating from that panic, I recognized it and gently reminded myself that the part of me who is observing my anxiety is not moved by my anxiety. I kept showing myself and my body, through my breath and my choices, that the worry could be there without running the day. From the outside, none of it seemingly fixed my business, solved my money problem, or made me feel like I was getting ahead. But I did find myself feeling lighter. I was smiling and laughing more in the last week than in the previous few months.

Sitting around the first fire, I pulled out my phone to take a picture of the finished product and noticed an email notification. It was a note from a leader of an organization I'd spoken at earlier in the year, and he was asking if I'd be open to doing coaching sessions with every member of their team. It turned out to be the largest coaching contract I'd signed to date and just as much money as the four speaking engagements that previously fell through.

I wish I could tell you that I saw that coming, but I didn't. And that's the point. Unstriving isn't a tactic for getting what you want on your timeline. It's a way of living that makes room for you to be fully human and fully alive once again. It lets you follow what's true for you even when it doesn't look efficient. It makes space for you to choose what brings you back to yourself, not just what keeps you ahead. Sometimes, life might respond with provision. Sometimes, it might respond with inner peace. Sometimes, it might respond with both. But either way, you're no longer living from the part of you that believes everything depends on your ability to force the outcome and hold it all together. You're living from something deeper and steadier. Something that doesn't disappear the moment things feel uncertain. You're in the river, and you know you can follow what's most alive in you and still be held. What a gift.

Transforming your life and how you show up in it doesn't happen all at once. It's built through a steady practice of beginning again. The miracle of this practice isn't that you will never strive again. The miracle is that every moment gives you another chance to live from the deeper truth you now know. To stop forcing. To trust the current. To remember that the life you are searching for is already here. And when you forget—when the noise rises, and the old fear grabs hold—just begin again.

About the Author

Paper Antler - Jonathan Hoffner

Caleb Campbell is a West Point graduate, former Army officer, and NFL athlete-turned-keynote speaker-and-author. After walking away from a life that looked like success on the outside, Caleb began a journey of inner transformation that redefined everything he believed about ambition, identity, and worth. Today, he speaks to organizations and audiences across the country who are running on empty, trying to meet relentless demands in a world that refuses to slow down. Through powerful storytelling and actionable insight, he helps them rise under pressure, expand what's possible, and make success feel good again. When not on stage, he spends time at home in Nashville, Tennessee, where he tries to convince his wife, Kara, that their daughter Sophie and son Rune need a Bernese mountain dog puppy.